# THE BROKER'S BIBLE

The Way Back to Profit for
Today's Real-Estate Company

## NANCY GARDNER

authorHOUSE®

AuthorHouse™
1663 Liberty Drive
Bloomington, IN 47403
www.authorhouse.com
Phone: 1-800-839-8640

First published by AuthorHouse 3/8/2011

ISBN: 978-1-4567-4494-6 (sc)
ISBN: 978-1-4567-4495-3 (e)

Printed in the United States of America

Any people depicted in stock imagery provided by Thinkstock are models,
and such images are being used for illustrative purposes only.
Certain stock imagery © Thinkstock.

This book is printed on acid-free paper.

*For my sons—Chip, Jay, Patrick, and John—
who have taught me what matters most.*

*And for the support of Nick and Jeannie and Carole.*

# Contents

# Introduction

According to a recent study by the *Harvard Business Review,* as well as a 2009 report in *TREND Magazine,* a consumer "crisis of trust" currently exists, extending to both government and business. This crisis is evident throughout the world but to a higher degree in this country. Just watch the news to see the ample evidence of this growing trend among the American people.

Real estate has long been a relationship business—basically it is a baby-boomer model—and as a result of this change in consumer confidence, the industry will no longer be able to thrive and prosper the way it has up to now. In other words, the relationship will no longer be able to stand alone as a way to secure business; going forward, it will be based on a combination of the relationship and verifiable skills—with the emphasis on *verifiable.*

The way we are measured has changed. The numbers are still the numbers, of course – but the difference is the ones that matter to the people that matter – the consumer who hires us – and the agents who consider working for us. A full understanding of this fact has to penetrate management mindset and objectives.

For today's skeptical consumer it's no longer market share.  No longer a claim to being "No. 1". No longer being the largest or oldest company in the area. In the eyes of the consumer these numbers can all be easily manipulated and often times are. In fact, these new 'measures' allow large and small companies to compete on a level playing field – these measurements speak volumes about our ability to get the job done.

The company's collective average (and an agents' individual) Days On Market; Listings Sold v. Listings Taken; Actual Sales Price v. original List Price as compared to the general market comprise our **competitive advantage** going forward.

These numbers prove your competitive advantage – and may be the only advantage that counts for a mistrustful consumer.

In addition is the fact that we are working through the most challenging and complex real-estate market and overall economic conditions since the Great Depression. "The recession has directly hit more than half of the nation's working adults, pushing them into unemployment, pay cuts, reduced hours at work or part-time jobs, according to a new Pew

Research Center survey." (*Washington Post,* 30 June 2010). High unemployment equals low numbers of home purchases.

Tight lending standards are also an obstacle to conducting business. Yes, lending institutions made plenty of loans that they should not have made; now these institutions deny plenty of loans that they should not deny. Lenders do not seem to be in business of lending anymore. Appraisal issues abound.

Shadow inventory continues to drive down prices—and, given their numbers (14 million nationwide at the end of 2009), they will continue to do so for the foreseeable future. As of April 2010, the national percentage of subprime mortgages in foreclosure (or at least 90 days delinquent) was 33 percent according to the *Wall Street Journal.*

Clearly, we in the real-estate industry have our work cut out for us.

However, in the midst of all this mess, enormous opportunity exists for real-estate companies, which now have the chance to move away from an agent-centered universe to a consumer-centered one. Such a shift will allow companies to be of service to the consumer in the ways that the consumer wants, needs, and is willing to pay for. Companies have to reinvent themselves around the consumer, not the agent. Furthermore, companies that do this will become the best places for any agent to work.

Let's discuss the obstacles to changing our modus operandi.

**Unskilled labor**—applies to both management and agents. Companies must question whether owners and brokers in charge have a firm grasp on their issues, and also whether they know how to implement what must be done in order to take corrective action. They must also question whether the clear leadership exists that will be required to implement such actions. In the event that brokers in charge don't have the requisite knowledge and are unwilling to acquire it, where does that leave the agents who are on the front line with the consumer? Most important, where does that leave the consumer, who is central to this new business model?

**Changes in consumer expectations**—remember that they now have access to the information real-estate professionals guarded so closely for so long. Consumers have options, and they have control. How much do real-estate professionals really know about what the consumer wants? Is the industry measuring what's important to consumers and responding to their answers in the delivery of services? If buyers and sellers are asked about the service and skill provided them, what percentage of those asked believe that real-estate agents earn the commission they charge? *That's* a question that should keep agents and management awake at night!

**Changes in measurements**—rather than relying on market share or being number one or a top producer, companies will now have to show that they and their agents have the necessary measurable skills. Companies and agents are now measured on their results statistics: days on market (for their listing inventory) as compared to the general market; percentage of listings sold vs. listings taken vs. the general market; percentage of actual sales price as compared to original list price. In order to earn credibility, trust, and loyalty, companies must pay attention to these statistics; these are the numbers that matter most to consumers, and they give companies a basis for the advice they proffer.

**Lack of standards, systems, structure, and control**—in short, this is a great way to run the asylum! Seriously, companies must make sure that they consider and correct the following issues: Is an updated and enforceable policy-and-procedure manual in place? Does the company require agents to meet a minimum production standard? Is training mandatory for both new and experienced agents, and is it relevant and dynamic? Without the necessary corrections to these issues, companies cannot expect success and profit. Brokers want change to occur from the outside (i.e., favorable market conditions; technology, etc.) If only the consumer were so easily satisfied!

**Lack of differentiation in the marketplace**—companies must ask themselves, "What sets us apart from our competitors?" This is often overlooked, yet it affects everything a company does. What program (map) is in place, which, when followed, ensures an agent's success—and as a result, the company's success? Can the company clearly communicate its value, above the competition, so that it can attract and retain the necessary talent from both the management and agent communities? Do both agents and consumers perceive what the company offers as a benefit?

**Agent teams**—are companies within companies. Does this bring profits to the company? Most brokers in charge have no idea how the team functions or who is responsible for what—that is, until a legal issue surfaces, and accountability comes to the foreground. The central issue to address and resolve is, Why do agents want to create teams in the first place?

In order to examine the issues addressed above and develop effective solutions, let us next look at three different real-estate companies.

## A Tale of Three Companies

[AUTHOR'S NOTE: *I cannot, in good faith, ask you to take my advice without giving you reasons to do so. I am about to tell you about three different companies and our work together. This happened in 2008—no market-driven success here.*]

Company ABC, an independent firm with two offices, started working with me in 2002. At that time, they had a six-figure loss, which continued through 2003. We had a lot of setbacks: poor branch management, personality issues, and their state's listing near the bottom in pricing.

We stayed with it. The managing owner continued to coach and recruit, and soon we saw his bottom line turn to profit. The company developed a marketing department that was second to none. It focused, not on print advertising, but rather, on marketing to SOI (sphere of influence) and using the Internet.

Early in 2008, another company approached ABC and made them an offer. By this time, their market had dropped 45 percent. ABC had more market share than their next three competitors combined. ABC's owner sold the company for a multiplier of five—almost unheard of today. When the owner announced the sale of the company to agents and staff, the only question they asked new management was, "Will the coaching program continue?" New management reassured them that the program would continue.

Company JKL was a franchise with four offices. I worked with the general manager who in turn worked with the four office managers. Only one of these managers fully implemented the program, and as a result, the profit for that office was up $150,000 over the previous year. The manager for this branch was new and had taken over for a much-beloved owner. The other three branches were working at large losses. Same company, same market conditions—but only the office that works the program is profitable.

Company XYZ, a franchise with three offices, worked with me for four years. When we started working together, they were not paying their bills. Two years later, all bills were current, and they had a nice cash reserve. At this point, the owner started to trip all over his ego. He visited another large company within his franchise and decided that acquiring real-estate companies was the way to grow his company. At the beginning of 2007, I terminated our working relationship, as his actions were against my advice. In spring of 2008, I started getting notices of their bankruptcy filing. I take no joy in this fact; these were wonderful people and I hated what happened with their business. I simply include this example to illustrate that the program works.

Three companies achieve three different results derived from decisions to follow the program—or not.

# 1

# The Generational Impact:
# Consumer and Agent

If real-estate companies want profitability, they must first understand the differences among today's consumers. A generational overview will help provide guidelines for ways to be adaptive to each generation and its preferences.

The differences among the generations have a twofold effect on the real-estate industry: They affect the consumers real-estate professionals seek to serve, and they affect the real-estate agents themselves. I am amazed at the small amount of training companies allocate to this area, which is so critical to customer satisfaction.

Adapting to the different generations is challenging for all involved. Every generation has its own preferences—not right or wrong, just different. It helps to have insights for understanding each of those differences.

Please bear in mind that approach is important—our brains are wired differently by means of all sorts of influences, including education, parental involvement, historical perspective, the economy, the ways we learned to get information, as well as how we communicate it.

## Traditionalists/Matures
**Born before 1945. Think *radio*.**

This generation is the last of civility in the world. Patient, respectful, and self-sacrificing—they were a part of World War II, if not directly, they felt the effects of the war at home as children. They set the course for modern America.

As consumers, Matures expect you to take the time to communicate directly with them. Do not rely on e-mail or text messages, and even voice mail can be tricky. Home ownership is a big deal to this group, and they believe it warrants the time and effort required. They are generally very amenable during negotiations, as most of them tend to be logical and fair-minded. They like organization, systems, and a rational approach with clear explanations. This is also a male-dominant group A more traditional role model is what you need to keep in mind when designing your approach.

As agents, the Traditionalists like a well-run office that has logical and fair policies and procedures. They are respectful to management, prefer a "top down" approach, and expect leadership to do the right thing. They understand doing the best for the most. They are loyal, long-term members of the team who are not as outspoken as their junior colleagues. They tend to take a more conservative approach and see technology as a necessary tool, but not an answer to everything. They want and expect training. As a rule, coaching does not work for them, but they prefer to be well trained.

## Baby Boomers
**Born 1945–64. Think *television*.**

Heaven knows when the majority of boomers will retire, as they are defined by their accomplishments, live to work, are materialistic, and tend to spend everything they earn. Boomers are great at building relationships—they had to be!, When they all hit the school system in such huge numbers—it was a baby boom, after all—educators had to find some way to manage all of them, so their "ability to get along well with others" became part of the grading system. Many boomers also shared textbooks, which presented another opportunity to control their behavior. Naturally socialized as children because most moms stayed at home, if they wanted to play with someone, they hit the screen door running and found plenty of other kids in the neighborhood who were more than happy to oblige.

The Vietnam War shaped boomers, as did other societal-changing events of that era, such as "witnessing" via television the assassinations of pivotal leaders, and observing women actually choosing to work outside the home and take control of their reproductive rights.

Boomers believed at that time—and most still believe today—that they can make the world a better place.

As consumers, boomers value relationships and will forgive a lot to keep them intact. They like being recognized by name, and they respond well to phone calls and voice mail—they will tolerate e-mail to a certain degree, as well as a limited amount of texting.

Because parents and teachers taught them to be sociable, they expect the same from those they work with—the relationship is the basis for everything. They understand that technology is necessary in today's world, and many of them have come to terms with its importance—about half of all boomers have assimilated technology to a level near to that of Generation X. With that said, people *still* matter the most to boomers—never forget that.

One caveat to all this: Do not, under any circumstance, think that the relationship will survive incompetence! It is more important than ever for agents to be knowledgeable as practitioners, given today's market conditions and the anger of consumers.

As agents, boomers love recognition and feeling that they are a part of an office identity. They view work as a social setting—both because they tend to spend a lot of time there and because of how important relationships are to them—so, the environment should be supportive. Boomers are generally loyal and team minded to a point, and they expect management to be knowledgeable and provide trusted leadership, as well as keeping things fun and directed. They highly value good training, but their response to coaching may only be lukewarm until they experience the benefits.

One thing that is important to note is that it will be interesting to see how well boomers transition into the new world of real-estate businesspeople. They must accept and understand that they have a job to do, based on their skills and their abilities. In other words, they will have to "get results" in a challenging marketplace, and the measurements of their performance will focus on their ability to get results instead of their ability to bond. In short, they will move from an all-personal relationship to a respected skill-based relationship backed up by the "numbers."

The last thing to remember about boomers is that, no matter how old they might be, boomers still consider themselves "cool"—keep that in mind when interacting with them as agents or consumers.

## Generation Xers
### Born 1964–80. Think *personal computer (PC)*.

This group is standing boomers on their collective ear. They are not typical of anything boomers ever encountered before—and with very good reason. Gen Xers are self-reliant and independent, and they come across as always looking out for "me." When you take into account that they were the first real generation of divorce, had working mothers, little adult supervision, and pretty much raised themselves, their traits are not hard to understand. They watched on TV as the *Challenger* exploded in mid-takeoff, they learned that they could die from having sex (AIDS), they lived through the Gulf War and its after effects, and they saw corporate and political leaders fall from power as a result of their own doing. In short, this crowd has no heroes. And because they saw their parents work themselves into divorce and disease, only to be downsized, they are not about to give everything to work. They want a good balance between work and home, and they strive to create the stable family life that they didn't have growing up. They are not a trusting group—no wonder, as the two people they loved the most couldn't keep their promises and ended up apart — why should they be?

As consumers, they expect everything yesterday. They grew up with remote controls (they're still the only ones that can program the thing) and PCs, and have fully integrated technology as part and parcel of their lives. They want correct information the first time, and they will make decisions accordingly. They don't trust relationships in the way that boomers do—you'll earn their trust by means of the knowledge, advice, and counsel you give them, as well as by following through on what you said you would do. Don't expect a personal relationship. They have friends. This is business. They expect networking as a part of conducting business. If you don't include them in your networking, don't expect to get their business because they "know" you. They are not as forgiving as boomers in that regard. If you want their business, work for it—and let your results speak for themselves. Again, they will choose based on what's in their best interest—not yours. It's just business.

As agents, Gen Xers expect knowledgeable management that can teach them how to earn the living they expect in this business. They want coaching (remember it's all about "me" for them) and believe that it's the best approach for increased production. This group does not "suffer fools," so don't waste their time. Training must be up-to-date, relevant, and delivered by someone who knows what he or she is talking about. Training videos should be available for review, understanding that the video is no substitute for a dynamic, relevant, and knowledgeable trainer. Some believe that Gen Xers want to do everything on their own. I disagree. They *do* value training requirements, *if* the training is worth their time. Once you have earned their respect and trust in this regard, getting them to attend is not an issue. When coaching a Gen Xer, you should focus on the attainment of their goals and increasing their freedom. Keep in mind that their time is valuable (think time away from loved ones), and if you show them ways to maximize their efficiency and effectiveness, they will value you.

*Rifts often develop between Boomers and Gen Xers because of the ways in which their approach and commitment to work varies. Boomers typically arrive late to the office, and then go to work on a flyer, which they proceed to walk around the office with, asking everyone within ear shot what they think. Font? Size? Info? After taking all day to get everyone's input, they finalize the flyer at day's end—in its original form. Contrast that with the Gen Xer who arrives at the office at normal business hours, goes about generating business, does all needed follow-up and follow-through, and is ready to go home before 4 p.m. In other words, the typical Gen Xer gets three times the work done in half the time, as compared with the typical boomer. Differing work ethic and commitment? I don't think so. It's simply that the Gen Xer doesn't need to spend the day socializing about a flyer, whereas the Boomer feels the social factor is primary. In truth, the Boomer's method is an outdated way to communicate information, but his or her attempt to seek group input is a well-intentioned one.*

## Millennials
### Born 1980–97. Think *Internet.*

It is also known as Generation Y, but I call this generation "digital in diapers." You'll find they can drive, talk/text on their cell phones, and listen to their iPods—all at the same time. If they can't "Google" you, you must be in the Witness Protection Program!

As a group, their childhood was affluent. They, too, are the children of divorce, and they learned to make the best of it—with multiple vacations, not to mention the bounty at birthdays and Christmas. This group did not carry the stigma of divorce; it was the norm. The way their parents divorced changed, too (i.e., joint custody). Often, parents lived in the same school district, and the child could live/visit with either. After-school involved lots of activities and plenty of socializing with play groups and sports teams. As a result, friends are very important to this group, often giving them what their families could not. By this time, parents had turned into helicopters, and the millennial child grew up in an environment that revolved around him or her.

They believe that they can do and have pretty much anything they set their hearts on—and Mom and Dad will back them to the end. They remain close to their families and often return home after college. *Why wouldn't they? They have great "space," complete freedom, great food, and no expenses, which leaves money to pay for their Beemers—if Mom or Dad has not paid for them already.* Surprisingly, this group appears to be politically conservative (don't think Democrat or Republican), environmentally aware, and socially involved.

As consumers, this bunch works through strong connections. If one person in their sphere worked with you and liked you; then all of them will. Here again, they highly value networking. They may choose to work with you because their parents did, but don't make the mistake of treating them like children—you'll lose them if you do. Consider them peers and treat them as you would any respected client. They expect you to know and use technology, and you had better be willing and able to text on a regular basis. Websites, smart phones, and laptops are a given, as well as a presence on social media sites. Think *connected* to the *n*th degree.

As agents, Millennials tend to expect to earn a lot of money quickly, and they want to feel they are making a contribution. Coaching and strong training are a must. They expect flexibility, and a dress code may present a challenge.

*I once had an agent argue that wearing a top that showed her midriff and navel decoration; designer jeans and expensive heels should be perfectly acceptable work attire because they were all very expensive—like I said, it's a challenge.*

# 2

# Budget Metrics That Matter Most

The "numbers" are important—they measure. A few key areas tell most of the story, so if you familiarize yourself with these each month, you'll have a clear picture of your strengths and weaknesses, and also where you need to focus your corrective efforts.

## Average Sales Price

- **Divide Total Volume by Number of Closed Sides**

  A decline in average sales price will quickly affect your bottom line. Company dollar will decline as well as profit. From a management perspective, you will need to increase the number of closed transactions just to keep up. Be aware of whether your agent population is focused on the number of deals closed or on making a certain amount of money. If prices are declining, agents will have to close more transactions to reach their desired income level. This will also impact you if you are counting on income from affiliated services based on the number of closed units.

## Per-Person Production

- **Divide Total Closed Sides by Total Number of Agents**

  The goal is to have all agents producing consistently. Make sure that the increase is not due to one or two top producers having a stellar year, as your bottom line won't reflect the increase because you will pay those agents more. As you coach and train agents, this number should increase, and it is a good measure of your effectiveness in those areas.

## Average Commission Rate

- **Divide Gross Commission Income by Total Volume**

This number indicates commission reductions. This can also occur if you are involved in a large number of new-home sales. More likely, your agents are reducing commissions or you are receiving less for co-broke sales. Check your company policy on this. Either enforce the existing policy or put a new policy in place, and use objection-handling training to prevent further reductions. A drop of even a few tenths of a percent in this number can negatively impact your bottom line significantly.

## Percent Company Dollar

- **Divide Net Commission Income by Gross Commission Income**

This percentage reflects the amount of money you retain after paying agents their commissions, but before you pay expenses. As a general rule, a healthy range here is between 32–36 percent. This range exhibits a good balance between what you pay your agents and what you retain (to pay bills and make a profit). If you are in this range and not making money, your production must be increased. If your percentage is lower and you still make good profit, this can be accounted for by the fact that you have a high sales volume.

## Percent Profit of Company Net

- **Divide Profit by Net Commission Income**

I advise that this should be a minimum of 15 percent—after you have paid everyone else, this is what's left over for you. Consider all the key numbers listed here in order to change this. Remember, you are entitled to a profit for the work you do.

## Review Expenses

- **Compare Current Year to Previous Year and Budget**

Compare categories of current year to those of previous year, looking for any changes. Compute expenses as a percentage of your net commission income.

If production and revenue are down, cutting expenses is less painful, as you do not need the same level of support. If you have to cut staff, try reducing hours all around rather than eliminating a position, if possible.

## Break-Even Point

- **Know the Bottom Line**

  Know the average amount you earn from each closed transaction. Know the number of transactions you must close each month to break even. Know the average number of closed transactions you'll need each month in order to reach your profit goal for the year. Knowing these numbers will keep you focused on what must be done each month. Otherwise, you're shooting in the dark. Divide net commission income by total number of closed transactions to compute amount of gross profit per deal. Divide total expenses by total number of transactions to determine cost per deal. Divide bottom-line profit/loss by total number of transactions to determine profit/loss per deal.

# 3

# Business Planning

## The Best Way to Predict Your Future Is to Create It

The plan is your map. Follow it, and it will guide you through any type of market conditions to your goals. Review your plan at least monthly and adapt as needed.

Where do you start? Think of the plan the same way you'd eat an elephant: one bite at a time.

Take each area of your company and decide what you want it to look like a year from now—if you are willing to do the work required and to learn along the way, you can create it.

Take the company apart one section at a time: Create the numbers for profit first, and then support those numbers with what you'll do in recruiting, coaching, training, customer service, staff support, and technology in order to reach them.

Surprisingly, most of what is required will add no additional expense; rather, it is a matter of the work you focus on Monday through Friday. Review your progress often and take an adaptive approach when necessary.

Along with the 2011 Company Business Plan example and the following explanations, you'll find additional comments about the plan in italics throughout the text.

## Explanation of the Plan

The first page has the numbers: past, present, and future. Remember, the numbers tell a valuable, necessary story. Take the time to fill out this part of the plan—next time it will be much easier. The numbers provide the measurements for your progress. If you're not "good with numbers" (welcome to the real-estate industry), you're not alone. Start now, and you can change that—you can learn anything with the right amount of effort and determination. Once you've mastered them, you'll be amazed at how little time you actually need to spend on numbers each month in order to have a clear sense of where you are.

**Be careful to measure numbers exactly**—set your decimal points to account for the smallest fractions. Report them accurately, as small discrepancies can account for thousands of dollars.

> *I was working with a large multi-office company and they were upset to see a significant decline in expected profits ($268,000). Analyzing the numbers found the reason for the decline. Average commission rates had dropped a very small percentage, and that cost the company six figures.*

**Fill out the rest of the plan**—the questions cover the major areas of running your company. Again, think in terms of how it's working now, versus what you want it to be this time next year.

**Think before you write**—if you are unwilling to commit to the work required behind your plan, it's a wish and nothing more. Just as you will teach your agents what must be done Monday–Friday in order to accomplish their goals and priorities, you must do the same.

**As you go through the plan, assign time frames for each of your priorities for the coming year**—you still have a company/office to run. The business plan is a live document that you will work from for the next twelve months. Some things you will begin right away (like establishing an agent coaching program after you've met with them to discuss their business plans); others things like adding a profit center may be planned for rollout in June. A business plan reflects what is to be done during twelve months, not one month. List any sizable budget items you are planning, along with a level of profit that must be achieved in order to pay for them. In a production downturn, you must plan for the opposite.

Form follows.

# 2011 COMPANY BUSINESS PLAN

Company _____

| | 2009 Actual | 2010 Actual | 2011 Goals |
|---|---|---|---|
| Listings Taken | | | |
| Listings Expired/Canceled | | | |
| Current Listing Inventory | | | |
| Current Listings Pending | | | |
| Listings Closed | | | |
| | | | |
| Buyer/Broker Agreements | | | |
| Current Buyer Pendings | | | |
| Buyers Closed | | | |
| | | | |
| Total Closed Units | | | |
| | | | |
| Total Sales Volume | | | |
| Average Sales Price | | | |
| Average Commission Rate | | | |
| | | | |
| Gross Commission Income | | | |
| Franchise Fees | | | |
| Other Income | | | |
| Agent Commissions Paid | | | |
| Net Commission Income | | | |
| Expenses | | | |
| Profit/Loss | | | |
| | | | |
| Per-Person Production (units) | | | |
| Closed Outbound Referrals | | | |
| Closed Inbound Referrals | | | |
| Home Warranties | | | |
| Closed Commercial Units | | | |
| | | | |
| Mortgage Capture Rate | | | |
| Settlement Capture Rate | | | |

Lay out your competitive advantage in today's market. Are you transparent in your communication with your agents about how/why you are making changes? Are you integrating levity?

List all your accomplishments in 2010. Is there anything in progress that you will continue to work on in 2011?

What is the total number of 2010 closed transactions done by the top 10 percent of your agents? % of LS versus LT for the office?

How many transactions will you need to close monthly in order to reach your 2011 profit goal?

Source of business—indicate the number and percentage of closed transactions generated from each source:

|  | Actual | | Percentage |
|---|---|---|---|
| SOI | _____ | = | _____ % |
| Marketing Effort | _____ | = | _____ % |
| Office/Company | _____ | = | _____ % |
| Internet | _____ | = | _____ % |

Generational breakdown of your customers:

|  | Percentage |
|---|---|
| 66+ | _____ % |
| 47–65 | _____ % |
| 31–46 | _____ % |
| 14–30 | _____ % |

**Recruiting**

List the agents hired (include terminations), noting whether each was new or experienced, as well as company dollar added by each in 2010. Also, list their generational breakdown. Do not count any new hire until he or she has had a closing.

What are your recruiting goals for 2011?

First, set your goal in the amount of additional company dollar generated: _____

Second, set the goal for the number of additional agents needed:      _____
    Number of experienced agents:          _____
    Number of new agents:          _____
    Number of terminations:          _____

How are you using your website and social media to recruit? What response are you getting?

What do you believe is your competitive advantage in recruiting?

**Agent Development/Coaching**

What are your coaching priorities for 2011?

How many of your agents will you meet with in 2011? List agents by last name and frequency of meetings. What is your plan to increase your coaching program in 2011? Again, list by name and frequency.

| | 2010 | 2011 |
|---|---|---|
| Weekly | | |
| Biweekly | | |
| Monthly | | |
| Not at all | | |

What help do you need to improve the coaching meetings? Have you applied the generational differences to your coaching?

Do you do a good job of recognizing your agents on an individual basis? Outline the recognition given.

**Training**

What are your training priorities for 2011? Include basic training for new- and experienced-agent workshops. How will you structure these in order to differentiate your company? How will you measure that agents consistently implement your training? How often will you conduct classes? How have you applied the generational information to your training? Have you planned script practice planned? What about social media?

Are you satisfied with attendance?

What are you doing to ensure that the consumer is getting the service they want from your company?

What areas of training do you delegate?

**Miscellaneous**

Assess your office staff on their levels of efficiency and effectiveness. Have they received cross-training? Do you hold regular staff meetings? What changes/improvements are you planning in 2011?

List any sizable budget expenses/cuts you are planning in 2011.




List any technological upgrades planned.




List any additional profit centers you plan to develop in 2011.




What will you do in 2011 to increase the level of direct contact between company and consumer?




What improvements will you make to core services?




List your profit per deal, per loan, and per closing in 2010.




What are you planning to do to increase agent benefits ("golden handcuffs")?

What do you see as the biggest changes/challenges you will face as a company in the next two years? How are you preparing?

What do you anticipate will be your greatest challenges in implementing your plan throughout the year?

How much vacation time are you planning for 2011?

**Technology**

Explain your technology package . What requirements do you have for your agents in terms of technology (i.e, smart phones and laptops)?

What system of follow-up/follow-through do you use for your leads management? What criteria must an agent meet in order to be eligible for leads? How often do you role play "Leads Mastery" training?

Have you updated your website to include monthly market stats? Do you use the monthly market stats for e-mail leads management? What website updates do you have planned for 2011?

What are you doing to improve your web knowledge/skills?

## Company Mid-Year Review

Here, the numbers represent actual results as compared to your goals for the year. Diagnose strengths and weaknesses, and then take corrective action. The best plans are adaptive.

# 2011 MID-YEAR REVIEW

Company _____

| | 2010 Year End Actual | 2011 Mid-Year | 2011 Goals |
|---|---|---|---|
| Listings Taken | | | |
| Listings Expired/Canceled | | | |
| Current Listing Inventory | | | |
| Current Listings Pending | | | |
| Listings Closed | | | |
| | | | |
| Buyer/Broker Agreements | | | |
| Current Buyer Pendings | | | |
| Buyers Closed | | | |
| | | | |
| Total Closed Units | | | |
| | | | |
| Total Sales Volume | | | |
| Average Sales Price | | | |
| Average Commission Rate | | | |
| | | | |
| Gross Commission Income | | | |
| Franchise Fees | | | |
| Other Income | | | |
| Agent Commissions Paid | | | |
| Net Commission Income | | | |
| Expenses | | | |
| Profit/Loss | | | |
| | | | |
| Per-Person Production (units) | | | |
| Closed Outbound Referrals | | | |
| Closed Inbound Referrals | | | |
| Home Warranties | | | |
| Closed Commercial Units | | | |
| | | | |
| Agents Recruited | | | |

List the amount of average company dollar earned on each transaction. How many transactions do you need each month to break even? What is your per-person production (PPP)?

Review your office/company recruiting objectives for this year. List accomplishments as of June 30.

Total number of agents:                    Total number of terminations:
Number of new hires:                       Number of experienced hires:

Number of days it takes a new hire to produce:

Amount of company dollar YTD from 2011 recruits:

**Agent Development**

Evaluate your coaching skills on a scale of 1 to 10 (1 = nonexistent; 10 = superior).

Understanding the Numbers                 _____
Writing an Agent Business Plan            _____
Coaching Time Management                  _____
Developing an Agent Schedule              _____
Determining Agent's Skill Level           _____
Working the SOI Annual Plan               _____
Using the Goals Worksheet                 _____
Adapting to Personality Style             _____
Determining Motivation                    _____
Determining Efficiency Level              _____
Determining Positive Motivation           _____
Determining Negative Motivation           _____
Determining Level of Empathy              _____
Determining Level of Drive                _____
Varying Level of Accountability           _____

Adapting to Generational Expectations      _____
Staying on Track      _____
Getting Price Reductions      _____
Using Dialogues      _____
Coaching Systems/Organization      _____
Consistency of Coaching Meetings      _____
Number of Agents Coached Regularly      _____
Social Media and Blogging      _____

What is your (company) average DOM for your listing inventory? What is your (company) percentage of LS to LT?

What are your training objectives for the last half of this year?  What issues are you targeting? Attach your training schedule.

Attach the agent production report YTD, noting how often you coach each of them.

Attach YTD profit and loss.

List your greatest challenges in plan implementation this year and list your priorities for the last half of 2011. What actions are you prepared to take?

## Agent Business Plan

Any business plan has three parts: goals, skills, and the work that must be done Monday–Friday in order to accomplish the goals. Failure to address all of these will result in failure of the plan.

Most agents hate business planning (as does management); as a result, most agents will tell you what they think you want to hear, and then forget about it.

The truth is, most people don't really know what they want out of life, and so they don't see how work can help them accomplish it. It takes time, but it is well worth the effort to help someone finally tap into what is really behind what they do every day.

Without a plan and goals, it will be difficult for management to provide the support that will be necessary for most agents to accomplish what they set out to do.

### Preparation

Create a schedule for your reviews. Decide the best times of each day for you to meet based on **your** schedule. Publish the meeting schedule and note that any agent who cannot meet during the appointed time frame should switch with someone else in the schedule and notify you.

Meet with each of your agents for an hour, and schedule no more than three or four reviews a day. You still have an office to run—more than that amount of reviews will put you into a stupor for certain.

Print out the agents' current production reports to help them with their numbers—they can add anything that will close by year-end.

Complete the reviews between Thanksgiving and Christmas, and you'll begin the New Year fresh and focused.

# 2011 AGENT BUSINESS PLAN

Agent Name _____

| | 2010 Actual | 2011 Goal |
|---|---|---|
| Listings Taken | _____ | _____ |
| Listings Expired/Canceled | _____ | _____ |
| Current Listing Inventory | _____ | |
| Current Listings Pending | _____ | |
| Listing Sides Closed | _____ | _____ |
| Buyer Broker Agreements | _____ | _____ |
| Current Buyer Pendings | _____ | |
| Buyer Sides Closed | _____ | _____ |
| Total Closed Sides | _____ | _____ |
| Average Sales Price | _____ | _____ |
| Total Sales Volume | _____ | _____ |
| Average Commission Rate | _____ | _____ |
| Agent Income | _____ | _____ |
| Mortgage Referrals | _____ | _____ |
| Home Warranties | _____ | _____ |
| Settlement/Escrow Services | _____ | _____ |

How do you feel about what you accomplished last year?

Why did you set your 2011 goals? What challenges do you anticipate in reaching your goals? How much vacation time will you take?

Rate your listing presentation on a scale of 1–10:

| | |
|---|---|
| Pre-Appointment Questions | _____ |
| Marketing Proposal | _____ |
| Pricing/Absorption Rate | _____ |
| Advice/Counsel | _____ |
| Consistent Follow-up | _____ |
| Seller Objections/Questions | _____ |
| Backup Mortgage Approval | _____ |

% of LS to LT                                   _____ (actual %)

Source of 2010 Listings :

| | | | | |
|---|---|---|---|---|
| SOI/Referral | _____ | = | _____ | % |
| Office | _____ | = | _____ | % |
| Marketing Effort | _____ | = | _____ | % |
| Internet | _____ | = | _____ | % |

Rate your buyer presentation on a scale of 1–10:

Pre-Appointment Questions       _____

Mortgage Approval/Backup       _____

Interview       _____

Absorption-Rate Analysis       _____

Representation       _____

Advice/Counsel       _____

Consistent Follow-up       _____

Buyer Objections/Questions       _____

Buyer Representation Agreement       _____

Source of 2010 Closed Buyers:

| | | | |
|---|---|---|---|
| SOI/Referral | _____ | = | _____ % |
| Office | _____ | = | _____ % |
| Marketing Effort | _____ | = | _____ % |
| Internet | _____ | = | _____ % |

List the generational breakdown of your clients in 2010:

66+   _____%    31 – 46   _____%

47 –65   _____%    14–30   _____%

What additional training will help you improve your business?

What do you think today's consumer wants from real-estate professionals? What will you do to deliver a higher level of customer satisfaction in 2011? What technological upgrades are you planning?

How will you market yourself in 2011? What is your budget?

How many times did you contact your SOI in 2010? Did you work from your SOI Annual Plan? Describe your leads-management system. How are you using social media/networks?

What do you believe you contribute to the company? Please list three specific contributions.

1.

2..

3.

## SOI MONTHLY MARKETING PLAN

Lay out your plan to network your SOI in 2011:

| | |
|---|---|
| January | |
| February | |
| March | |
| April | |
| May | |
| June | |
| July | |
| August | |
| September | |
| October | |
| November | |
| December | |

Is your SOI database <u>systematized</u> and updated to include all of the following: address, phone number, work number, cell phone, e-mail address, and social media?.

## GOALS WORKSHEET –
## DAILY WORK PLAN

| | | |
|---|---|---|
| 1. Annual Income Goal | | |
| 2. Average Income per Transaction | | |
| 3. Number of Transactions Needed | (1 ÷ 2) = | |
| 4. 10% Number in SOI | | |
| 5. Number of Additional Transactions | (3 - 4) = | |
| 6. Number of Additional Contacts (200 contacts to close a deal) | (5 x 200) = | |
| 7. Number of Weeks Worked This Year (subtract number of weeks to close) | | |
| 8. Number of Contacts Each Week | (6 ÷ 7) = | |
| 9. Number of Days Worked Each Week (5) | | |
| 10. Number of New Contacts Daily (i.e., JLJS, FSBOs, Expired) | (8 ÷ 9) = | |
| 11. Number of SOI Contacts (SOI/20) | | |
| 12. Total Number of Contacts Each Day | (10 + 11) = | |

*Schedule* the time you will need to make your contacts each day (M–F), based on an average of ten to twelve contacts per hour.

## Agent Mid-Year Review

This is the most important review of the year. It is real world. No empty promises—you are seeing the results of half a year's efforts. You are looking at commitment. You are looking at skill level. Now go to work.

This review tells the story, and it can be an opportunity for the agents to see management as integral to their success.

From their real mid-year numbers, as opposed to the fabrications on their business plans, you can begin to diagnose issues.

What do they tell you about commitment? Work habits? Skill level? Strengths and weaknesses? Consistency? What training do they need? Did the agents stay on track and follow their SOI Annual Plans? How can you be of help to them?

Mid-year is also the time to adjust goals—if it is unlikely that agents will attain their goals at this point, it is better to adjust their goals to something the agents can reach. Reaching a goal carries with it momentum, and that can help agents start the next year off on a higher note. Refigure the "Goals Worksheet" for the last half of the year.

# 2011 AGENT MID-YEAR REVIEW

Agent Name _____

|  | 2011<br>Mid-Year Actual | 2011<br>Goal |
|---|---|---|
| Listings Taken | _____ | _____ |
| Listings Expired/Canceled | _____ | _____ |
| Current Listing Inventory | _____ | _____ |
| Current Listings Pending | _____ | _____ |
| Listing Sides Closed | _____ | _____ |
| Buyer/Broker Agreements | _____ | _____ |
| Current Buyer Pendings | _____ | _____ |
| Buyer Sides Closed | _____ | _____ |
| Total Closed Sides | _____ | _____ |
| Total Sales Volume | _____ | _____ |
| Agent Income | _____ | _____ |
| Mortgage Referrals | _____ | _____ |
| Home Warranties | _____ | _____ |

How do you feel about what you have accomplished so far this year? What are your priorities at this point? What actions will you take?

Lay out what you have done to work your SOI year to date *Be specific.*

January _____

February _____

March _____

April _____

May _____

June _____

What is your percentage of LS to LT? What is your average DOM for your current listing inventory? What is your percentage of actual sales price to original list price for your LS in 2011?

How are you developing a following on social media? How often do you update?

Define source of your business by the generations; use percentages.

| | | | |
|---|---|---|---|
| Matures (66+) | _____ | Boomers (47–65) | _____ |
| Generation Xers (31–46) | _____ | Millennials (14–30) | _____ |

Rate yourself on a scale of 1–10 in the following areas:

Listing Presentation      _____

Marketing Listing      _____

Absorption-Rate Pricing      _____ (S)      _____ (B)

Backup Mortgage Approval      _____

Seller Objections      _____

Seller Advice/Counsel      _____

Price Reductions      _____

Buyer Presentation      _____

Buyer Advice/Counsel      _____

Buyer Objections      _____

Lead Follow-up System      _____

Closing Skills      _____

Negotiating      _____

Contract/Legal Issues      _____

Contract to Closing      _____

Working with Staff      _____

Customer Service      _____

Working SOI      _____

Website/Webpage      _____

E-mail Response      _____

Time Management      _____

Generational Differences      _____

Using Social Media      _____

Source of 2011 listings:

SOI/Referral      _____ = _____ %

Office      _____ = _____ %

Marketing Effort      _____ = _____ %

Internet      _____ = _____ %

How many of your current listings are over 60 days?

Source of 2011 closed buyers:

SOI/Referral      _____ = _____ %

Office      _____ = _____ %

Marketing Effort      _____ = _____ %

Internet      _____ = _____ %

Lay out your plan to work your SOI through the rest of the year(by phone, in person, by e-mail, social media and mail):

July          _____

August        _____

September     _____

October       _____

November      _____

December      _____


Is there anything else you would like to address?

# 4

# Hiring Sales Management

Skilled management is more important than ever before in the real-estate industry. Management must be able to attract new talent, and then successfully develop those new agents, as well as nurturing existing agents. Great management functions like a magnet in the marketplace, and it is the most-important competitive advantage that a company offers.

Hiring strong management is an industry-wide challenge. Much of existing management today is doing one of two things: leaving the industry altogether or convinced that management has nothing new to learn. New management has little or no direction (it used to be: "make agents happy"), and soon they realize that they can make more money in sales, and with considerably less stress.

Today's industry and market call for serious work done by skilled people. Training for management is worse than it is for sales associates. Most managers don't ask for it, not wanting to expose the fact that they don't know what to do or don't want to do the work. I've often said that a good market covers a lot of sins—we have ample evidence of that today.

With that said, let's look at what to do in order to ensure hiring and retaining effective management.

## Job Description

### Expectations
Be clear about your expectations for management in the following areas:

**Profit**— the real job you hire management to do is to make the office profitable. Outline what you expect here—no one functions well in the dark.

**Recruiting**—how many agents do you want to hire and how much company dollar will these hires add to the bottom line? Align recruiting and profit expectations. Communicate the following very specifically: the number of new agents you want to hire, the number of experienced agents you want to hire, and how much you expect the bottom line to improve as a result of hiring them.

**Business Planning**—refers to the office business plan, which you must review monthly and update semi-annually, as well as to agent business planning, which you must do for all agents.

**Agent Coaching Program:**—for whom is this mandatory? What percentage of the agents do you expect to need coaching? How often?

**Training Program**—refers to company offerings versus branch offerings. Identify whether this is a program for new agents, experienced agents, or both. How often are the classes available? Is any of the training delegated? What is your expectation as to the manager's involvement in training classes?

**Accountability**—how often do you expect management to meet with the general manager/owner? What information do you intend to discuss at such meetings?

What kind of reporting do you expect? How often do you want to receive reports?

**Again, hiring effective management is critical today.** Before you begin interviewing, take the time to assess both what the office needs and the skills required to address those needs. Hiring mistakes are costly, and few companies have the financial resources, or the time, to bring in someone who is not up to the task—not to mention the threats to agent retention as an office stagnates.

A sample "Management Interview" follows—make sure you familiarize yourself with the questions. Be ready to probe for additional information as needed. Many candidates are good at interviewing and more than capable of telling you what you hope to hear. Ask *how* they will accomplish something—anyone can talk about objectives, but the ability to clearly state how to do it sets apart effective managers.

Write out their answers and put them in a file for future reference. You should have a separate file for each candidate interviewed. Review their answers after you have gained some distance from the interview; at that time, you can assess for actual substance, willingness, and ability to execute.

## Interviewing Management Candidates

*Begin with appropriate conversation to build rapport based on your knowledge of the interviewee.*

# MANAGEMENT INTERVIEW

Name:                                                    Date:

Describe what you believe to be the major responsibilities of a manager.

Why do you think you are suited to management?

What challenges do you envision in recruiting? What will you look for in an agent? How will you determine your recruiting goals?

What do you think agents look for in a manager?

Do you believe that all agents should work from a business plan? Do you believe management should put in place and enforce a minimum production standard? How important is coaching in developing an agent? Do you believe that all agents need to participate in the office coaching program? How would you approach agents in order to involve them in the program?

What type of training would you put in place for new agents? How often would you train? Do you think training should be mandatory for agents?

What training would you provide experienced agents? How would you get them to attend?

How important is building a culture to an office? How would you go about building a strong culture? How will you address generational differences in the office?

*Lay out a situation (i.e., "How would you handle . . ." and "What would you do if . . ."), and have the candidate explain his or her choice of action. Make sure the situation addresses current issues in your office.*

Are you computer/technology literate? How would you use technology in a real-estate office? For the agent? For recruiting? How are you using social media?

What systems do you believe should be in place to support agents in their work?

Why do you think an agent would want to work for this company?
Why do you want to work for this company?

What do you think today's agents are looking for in company?

How do you feel about working with a management trainer/consultant?

What would you change in the company if you were manager?

As manager of this office, what would your first priorities be?

What questions/concerns do you have at this point?

*If you are interested in this person, set a second interview and cover any remaining questions at that time.* **Go over what you expect from this manager. Be specific about how you will hold him or her accountable, and also how you will measure his or her performance..** *To reiterate,* **be very specific.** *Explain the compensation package for the position, as well as your bonus structure (which is based on a percentage of profit).*

## Accountability

Once you've made the decision to hire a manager, you must coach him or her regularly. You must also hold the new manager accountable to job expectations. I recommend that you hold these management accountability meetings the first and third weeks of each month. Provide an atmosphere where it is safe to learn—from mistakes and otherwise. Make sure the new manager performs the activities that you expect and that are necessary to profitability—the expertise will follow.

This management coaching form will help you stay on track, avoid schmoozing, and allow for the discussion that must occur between ownership and management. This discussion follows the job-description activities that are critical to profitability.

*[Form follows, with explanations in italics.]*

# MANAGEMENT COACHING FORM

First meeting of each month, go over monthly production numbers.

LT: _____     LS: _____     BS: _____     C/E: _____     Profit: _____
*listings taken / listings sold/ buyer side sales/ listings canceled/ listings expired*

How many recruiting appointments have you had since our last meeting?
_____ (new) _____ (experienced)

Agent names _____
_____ (new agent contacts) _____ (experienced contacts)
*Track by name to ensure consistency and avoid dropping leads.*
*If appointments are not on track, ask how many contacts have been made.*

What challenges are you having in recruiting?


How many agent coaching meetings have you held since our last meeting?
List weekly agents by name:



List biweekly agents by name:



What training classes have you held since our last meeting?



How many attended?




Any staff issues to address?




Follow-up on any assigned projects.




What can I do to help you?

## Compensation

In two words, it varies. Managers usually receive a base salary (this also varies, based on cost of living in your area and also on what your competition pays), plus a bonus incentive. The bonus is based on a percentage of profit, and that percentage increases as the profit increases. For example: 10 percent for the first $100,000; 20 percent for the next $400,000, and 30 percent for $500,000 and more. Always compute what that figure might be, given best- and worst-case scenarios—and make sure it's fair for all concerned. If they are getting results, pay them.

> *I once coached a manager to build what became a very successful and profitable office. After two consecutive years of sizable gains, the owner decided to cut the compensation of a very hardworking and results-oriented manager. Needless to say, she lost the manager and most of the agents as well. To this day, that company has not regained its footing—all as a result of that short-sighted decision.*

## Non-compete Clause

This is a must in any management contract today. Consult with your favorite attorney (who is well versed in this area) in order to find out how to integrate a non-compete into your management contract. It should include a time line and a measure of distance from the office, and the contract language must be to be enforceable in your state.

[**Note:** Some companies have also added a non-compete clause into new agents' independent contractor agreements—consult an attorney here, too—don't train and coach agents for your competitors!]

# 5

## Agent-Coaching Program

Why begin an agent coaching program? You may be thinking: "Haven't I got enough to do already?" In reality, how much of your time do you spend on the things that actually improve your bottom line, such as increasing agent production and improving retention? Do your agents see you as a strong component of their business? Do you function mainly as a deal doctor? How will you attract and keep the talent required in today's competitive market? Your involvement, one-on-one, in your agents' business is the highest level of broker support you can provide. Your agents will see you as an integral part of their success.

## Benefits of Coaching

- **Improves agent production** — increases their focus and keeps them on track.
- **Improves retention**—this is key, because if they see you as an integral part of their success, they will be far less likely to leave.
- **Improves value of management** — proves to be the highest level of support a broker can offer; it translates to real value, because it is your time with your agents, one-on-one.
- **Improves customer service** — a must focus on the customer while guiding the agent to improve; focusing on leads management and follow-up is the foundation of customer satisfaction. *This is critical for **all** companies going forward.*
- **Improves sales**— reduce canceled and expired listings; with regular focus on price reductions and assigned price reductions, you'll sell the listings you take.
- **Improves effectiveness**— decrease fall through – you'll spot weakness and correct.
- **Improves your control of the office**—your power is one-on-one; agents can hide in a group meeting.

Also consider these additional benefits:
**You'll actually enforce minimum production standards**—with regular meetings that monitor activities and production, you'll deal with this issue on an ongoing basis. You'll terminate non-producers sooner, which will enable you to spend more time focusing on agents who produce.

**You'll cut expenses**—if you teach agents to build business through SOI and/or the Internet, and Social Media, print advertising and flyers will go the way of the dinosaur.

**You'll drive business to your affiliated services**—you can question the reasons why agents may not use these services; listen carefully, because you'll gain information that is critical to the success of these services, and when they have improved, you can approach the agents to give them another try.

**You'll develop agents for life**—where else will agents get this level of support and valuable attention?

**You'll manage your time better**—regular, pre-scheduled appointments will cut down on your "got a minute?" interruptions, as agents will know that you know what's going on with them; as you train them to do their job better, fewer problems requiring your attention/action will surface.

**You'll give the agent recognition**—your time one-on-one is extraordinary recognition! You focus on the individual, build a better team (getting everyone onboard one at a time), and positively influence the agent mind-set and attitude. Remember, you'll develop agents for life, as loyalty improves through effective and meaningful coaching.

**You'll receive your own rewards**—nothing is better than your ability to increase agents' production and income through your coaching program. Some agents will reach levels they never thought possible because of the coaching *you* provided.

The question that remains is this: If coaching is so great, why don't we do it? Even those brokers who have received training on how to coach don't always do it—or they begin a coaching program for their agents, but before long, it unravels.

Here are a few of the reasons "why not" to coach that I've encountered over the years:

"I don't have time."
"I'm not sure I'd be good at it"
"I'm not good at writing plans, etc."

The list of reasons goes on and on, but you get the idea.

My response to each reason is the same: "You've got to start somewhere."

*One of my recent clients has increased company dollar from 19.6 percent to 26.8 percent. This took approximately eighteen months to accomplish. At mid-year 2010, this company had doubled its profit. Better yet, this company is now number one in every category in their MLS, in spite of their area's market conditions continuing to worsen.*

Here are some final thoughts on coaching.

Agents who know that they need more than management gives them will go outside the company for direction, focus, and guidance. Outside coaching is expensive, and it hands off the agent to someone else. Many managers seem relieved by this—until they recognize that their agents' loyalty now belongs to someone outside the company.

This is *your* job! You hired agents with a promise of support and production—it's your responsibility to keep that promise. The rest is up to them.

Your level of commitment is of critical importance—the agents will take their cue from you. If you don't show up or reschedule, so will they. If you get off track and schmooze during the meetings, they won't take it seriously, and neither they, nor you, will realize any benefit.

## Determine Which Agents to Coach

Which agents do you coach? All agents? Just the non-producers? Just the top producers? Will your coaching program be mandatory?

I recommend that you *offer* coaching to *all* your agents, but make it mandatory for the new agents (less than two years' experience) and for your low and non-producers. The new agents will thrive under your direction—they don't know what to do. The low/non-producers will either start to produce or drink coffee elsewhere! Coach these agents weekly.

You can coach the remainder of your agent population every two weeks.

Don't make the mistake of assuming your top people don't want coaching—they complain that management focuses only on the agents who aren't doing anything, with little leftover for the people "making it happen" every month. You may end up coaching many of your top agents monthly—even over lunch, in the beginning. Make sure you research their year-to-date production versus their goals and objectives for the year. Analyze for weaknesses, ask questions, and give direction accordingly. You can take more than one approach to get agents into a coaching program!

## Rollout of the Coaching Program

Proper implementation is critical to a successful program. Take the time to prepare what you will say to introduce the program to your people. Best time of year is usually at the beginning of a quarter. As with any initiative, stress the benefits; give the agents a "what's in it for me" incentive to get them onboard.

Getting started can be the toughest part, so I've included a sample dialogue for you to use to introduce coaching:

> *"We all know that market conditions continue to change—from the Internet, to the increasing expectations of mistrustful and angry consumers, to the economic downturn, to the lack of liquidity, etc. The point is, our business is more challenging than ever. Given all this, I want to assure you that, as the company adapts to these changes, the one thing that we want to be sure of is that each of you reaches the level of success and income that you want for yourself and your families each year.*
>
> *In order to ensure that you get what you set your sights on, we are implementing an agent coaching program.*
>
> *What is the agent coaching program? This is a time set aside on a regular basis when I will meet with each of you, one-on-one, to check in, discuss what you're doing, and address any challenges that you are encountering. It will be a time when I will help you stay focused, fine tune your efforts, weed out the "stuff" that is getting in your way.*
>
> *In a nutshell, this is about us helping you get what you want out of your business— whether that means taking it to a new level or maintaining what you are doing and helping you to get your personal life back—I am committed to helping you get what you want".*

Answer any questions, letting them know that a schedule will be published with dates and appointment times.

## Files and Scheduling

**Setting up your files**—I use composition folders with one divider in the center for each person that I coach. The left inside front cover holds past coaching forms for reference, and the right inside front cover holds blank coaching forms for future meetings. Use the back sections to display latest Business Plan, Goals Worksheet, and SOI Annual Plan for tracking purposes.

**Develop a schedule**—it is best to use time blocking with your coaching schedule. Plan on twenty minutes per session, which equals three meetings an hour. So, if you coach thirty agents per week, for a total of ten hours, plan two hours per day, and schedule them when you are at your best. Hold them consecutively, as this allows for better time management; in addition, you'll actually get into a "groove," which will help you hold better meetings. (Note: Agents will stay as long as you let them. At the end of the twenty-minute time frame, recap, and then stand up and say that it's time for your next meeting. You'll never cover everything they need, nor should you try to, as the agent will leave overwhelmed—and then will accomplish absolutely nothing.)

Allow no interruptions during coaching—short of the building burning down. The goal is to keep them on track, and make them better at what they do, as they realize their goals and objectives.

It is important to emphasize that *you* are the one in control of the meeting! Agents are aware of this, and some will try to undermine you. The first way most try to accomplish this is to move the discussion to the deals they are having problems with—make a separate appointment to discuss this, and stay on track with the form. If that fails, or if they are severely off track, they'll talk about personal issues. Some may have merit, but most don't. Advise counseling if appropriate; and, whatever you do, don't take sides. Counsel that staying on track with their business will at least give them control in one area of life.

Make good notes on the form so that you'll have the continuity and value needed for future meetings.

Have fun!

## Goals Worksheet

Fill out this form for each agent after you have reviewed the goals in his or her business plan. You should also fill one out anytime you need to adjust an agent's goals.

New agents (less than six months) use this form, along with the SOI Annual Plan, as their business plan and also as a guide for their daily activities. Consistency is critical at this stage, as the failure rate is high. Figure new agents for one transaction per month or align with your minimum production standard until production is consistent.

The "Goals Worksheet" is the tool you use to translate the plan into reality, Monday through Friday. It represents what an agent needs to do each day in order to produce to a certain level.

*[Forms follows.*

## GOALS WORKSHEET –
## DAILY WORK PLAN

| | | |
|---|---|---|
| 1. Annual Income Goal | | |
| 2. Average Income per Transaction | | |
| 3. Number of Transactions Needed | *(1 ÷ 2)* = | |
| 4. 10% Number in SOI | | |
| 5. Number of Additional Transactions | *(3 - 4)* = | |
| 6. Number of Additional Contacts (200 contacts to close a deal) | *(5 x 200)* = | |
| 7. Number of Weeks Worked This Year (*subtract number of weeks to close*) | | |
| 8. Number of Contacts Each Week | *(6 ÷ 7)* = | |
| 9. Number of Days Worked Each Week | *(5)* | |
| 10. Number of New Contacts Daily *JLJS, FSBOs, Expired)* | *(8 ÷ 9)* = | |
| 11. Number of SOI Contacts | *(SOI/20)* | |
| 12. Total Number of Contacts Each Day | *(10 + 11)* = | |

*Schedule* **the time you will need to make your contacts each day (M–F) based on an average of ten to twelve contacts per hour.**

## SOI Annual Plan

This form serves as the guide as to how an agent will contact his or her SOI every month of the year. Have all agents fill this out when they join your office—and again as part of their monthly plan. It is only necessary to fill in the phone, e-mail, social media and mail, etc., each month—you do not need to be specific as to the content of each at this point.

Watch for older agents who only want to mail to their SOI, and also for younger agents who want to take care of everything online. Agents must make at least one phone call per quarter in order to cement the relationship. The other approaches will vary according to the generational breakdown of their SOI.

Social media has emerged as another way to sustain SOI relationships. Agents must learn that the way to develop a following is by providing consistent and useful content—*not* by marketing or selling. (We will discuss this further in chapter 10, which focuses on technology, websites, and social media).

> *When I'm visiting an office site, I often see that agents have posted this "SOI Monthly Marketing Plan" form at their desks in order to stay focused on their approach for each month.*

*[Form follows.]*

## SOI MONTHLY MARKETING PLAN

*Lay out your plan to network your SOI in 2011 (i.e., in person; telephone contact; e-mail; postcard)*

| | |
|---|---|
| January | |
| February | |
| March | |
| April | |
| May | |
| June | |
| July | |
| August | |
| September | |
| October | |
| November | |
| December | |

Is your SOI database updated to include the following: address, phone number, work number, cell number, and e-mail and social media addresses?

Be sure to add to each contact: "If you happen to hear of anyone who might be thinking of buying or selling this year, I'd love the opportunity to help them. If I don't hear from you, I'll be in touch next month."

## Coaching Form

This form is a guide that will help you stay on track—and keep you from schmoozing. Fill out as much of the top part as you can for each agent, and then make copies of it for future meetings, so you don't have to fill it out each time.

Begin by addressing how consistently—or not—they work their SOI, and also how effectively—or not—they use their tracking system. **Stay here until you correct these issues.** Delegate time frames for completion and verify that they have completed whatever you assigned. If you don't do all this, you won't have much else to talk about, as they won't be doing any business. If you consider that SOI is the foundation for building and generating business—not to mention that it's what the consumer prefers—all this makes sense!

Track their listing appointments/listings taken, buyer appointments/buyer contracts, and leads management accordingly. Track leads by last name to ensure accuracy of follow-up, etc.

Be aware that you need to hold new agents and agents who do not meet your minimum production standard to higher accountability in regard to their SOI activities—this is the only way to improve their work habits and generate production.

The form has directives in italics to help in your coaching conversation—and the best coaching has a conversational quality that flows from one topic to the next. It takes time and experience to master this. Allow yourself—and your agents—the time to learn.

Use the form to interview the agent. Do not give it out beforehand, or you will end up with "cooked" numbers. Better to have the discussion—you'll learn much more.

*[Form follows.]*

# AGENT COACHING FORM

2011 Income Goal _____ Why? _____

2011 Goal – Closed Transactions _____ # in SOI _____

Closed Transactions YTD _____ # Transactions Pending _____

Source of Business

%LS _____                 DOM _____

---

*"Let's take a look at what you are doing."*

How are you contacting your SOI this month?

*Refer to the SOI monthly plan for directive here. Make sure they are following it, and then look at next month and help them organize for the next contact.*

How many listing presentations have you had since our last meeting? _____

Seller names: _____  _____  _____  _____

How many listings did you take? _____

*If they are going on appointments but not getting the listings, probe each name, find out what happened, and then coach the desired result.*

Listing Inventory _____      Price Reductions Needed _____

*As you see the need, check for needed reductions, review dialogue, and assign them.*

How many Buyer showings have you had since our last meeting? _____

Did you sign them to Buyer Agency agreements? _____

Buyer names: _____  _____  _____  _____

Have they been pre-approved for mortgages? Backup approval? _____

*If not, question as to why, etc., and then coach the importance of doing so.*

How many leads do you have that will buy or sell within the next month?

Sellers: _____                 Buyers: _____

*Refer back to this to make sure that they follow- up. If they are not, check their follow-up system and the dialogue they are using. Correct as needed.*

How are you doing balancing work and home?

*Look for opportunities to ease them into better time management. Start them on a routine for the early part of the day, making sure they schedule what must be done to build consistent business early in the day.* _____

*Recap with any questions for them for what you expect them to do. End the meeting on an upbeat note, and then confirm the next meeting appointment.*

## Analyzing the Agent

**Skill level** —determine each agent's strengths and weaknesses. Coaching agents is not one-size-fits-all; it varies based on the skills and motivation levels of the agent. Time in the business does not necessarily mean skill; many stay around just to drink your coffee and talk about the bad market.

Consider the skill level of each agent that you will coach. What is his or her production level? Is production up/down from previous years? What kind of work habits does he or she have? Does he or she use absorption-rate pricing analysis on listings? What is the average DOM (days on market) for his or her listing inventory? What percentage the agents' listings sell? Has he or she mastered a professional listing and buyer presentation? Does he or she handle consumer objections well, or does he or she treat such objections as a reason to fail? Does he or she attend training? Is he or she adaptive to today's consumer? How does he or she use technology? Does he or she have an Internet strategy? Using Social Media?

*Rate each of them on a level of weak, fair, or competent in these categories.*

**Motivation matters**—this is tough to determine for a lot of people. We don't seem to be able to figure out what we want. Coaching is a lot easier when you know what makes an agent get out of bed every day. Keep probing; it will show up. Be aware that if they are in a survival mode, they will not be able to get beyond that until they can pay their bills. Positives motivate some people; negatives motivate others. It's not right or wrong—just different—and it has nothing to do with being an optimist or a pessimist. Positively motivated people respond best to their accomplishments. Negatively motivated people respond to fear and loss—not surprisingly, many top producers fall into this category. Their top status as an agent defines many of them.

**Empathy**—how strong are the agents' people skills? Are they able to put themselves in someone else's shoes and still get the job done? Don't confuse empathy with sympathy—the difference between them is huge.

**Personality style**— salespeople have received a lot of instruction on personality styles. Tony Alessandra's *The Platinum Rule* is second to none on this topic. I highly recommend this thorough book. Take the test and you'll learn to understand yourself first, which is key to effectively communicating with others. We all talk a lot, but how much of what we mean to say is what we actually communicate? How much does the other person understand? In short, the ability to adapt gets the job done.

## Probation

If all else fails—you have coached and trained the agent consistently for a period of ninety days, yet no productivity has resulted. This agent lacks motivation and/or skill, and he or she simply does not belong in sales. Put this agent on a period of probation that focuses on activities and includes daily accountability. If he or she still fails to follow any of the directives, then it's time to terminate.

### Terms of Probation

First, re qualify the agent's desire to stay with company—what is the sense of going forward if he or she wants out? *"Do you still want to work in real estate? With this company?"*

If this agent still wants to work in real-estate sales, put the following terms in writing for both of you to sign and date:

- Agree to thirty-day probation period
- Agree to weekly coaching
- Agree to attend all training sessions
- Agree to attend all sales meetings
- Agree to work their SOI and Social Media and to leave you a voice mail detailing the number of contacts made each day

If agent fails to complete any of the above items, you have grounds for immediate termination.

[**Note:** If the agent does the work outlined and does not get results, he or she has a skill problem and needs more training. Listen to this agent make his or her contacts, and you'll quickly diagnose the weakness. Use reality dialogues (role play) to correct. Again, if the agent does not do the work outlined, he or she lacks motivation, and you need to terminate.]

## Minimum Production Standard

For many, this is the basis for their coaching program. Every company should have one—and ***it must be enforceable.*** I ask this question of all my new clients, and they always tell me that they do indeed have a program, but they do not enforce it. It is better not to have one than to have one that you do not enforce. Simply put, not enforcing programs will undermine your credibility. Your agents will say, *"Yes, that's what they say, but not to worry, they never enforce it."*

**Pick a number …**I recommend that you create a standard that you can enforce—you have bills to pay. Begin with a number, say twelve, and then look at your roster for the last six-month period. You'll see how many agents you'd have to terminate if the standard were in place today. If you can't/won't terminate those agents, then you need to lower your standard, until you arrive at a number that you can and will enforce.

No "rule" exists that says that you can't raise the standard once your coaching and training programs are underway; you can raise your hiring standards at that point, too. It is better to have a minimum standard of six transactions per year enforced than a standard of twelve that you do not enforce.

# 6

# Agent-Recruiting Program

I don't think there has ever been a time when recruiting has been more important – and it's always been important to our future. We face so much uncertainty – no one knows where this economy is headed for sure. Our strategy has to be to do more of the business that's being done – no matter the market.

The question looms: how do we attract them when so many brokerages are offering extraordinary commission splits – to add production at any cost. Add to that the fact that there is a growing gap between productive agents and marginally productive agents and what that means for your company is a shrinking company dollar.

Again your 'numbers" will sell your story. If your training and coaching are worthwhile – you numbers will demonstrate this fact in your production. The stats that will comprise your competitive advantage in recruiting are DOM; %LS v LT; Actual Sales Price v Original List Price; add to those your PPP; and # days it takes a new hire to produce; and the % increase in production of any experienced agent that has enjoyed since joining your company. – all of these support the effectiveness of your programs. Business Planning, Agent Coaching, Dynamic Training, strong Technology support and direction plus great staff comprise your competitive advantage going forward – the rest of it, everybody else has.

An old sales adage says, "Recruiting solves all of your problems." Does it really? It can—based on the quality of the people you hire, as well as what happens to them once they join your company.

## Qualities of a Good Hire

Consider this – the real estate industry has historically hired based on personality and people skills – will these traits get the job done today? Our markets are more complex and a thorough comprehension of statistics and how they affect buying and selling is critical. Think about what's needed in the marketplace today, when you hire your next agent. A hiring standard is critical to strong and productive recruiting. What qualities do you want? It's much easier to hire if you know what you are looking for in advance.

## List the Qualities You Want in Your Agents

**Strong SOI and a willingness to work it**—the ability to network both online and offline is key; you cannot underestimate it. People prefer to work with people they know and believe they can trust. SOI is the basis from which we build our business. How will agents without a sphere of influence build their business? I am not saying it's impossible, but it does take longer—and it requires strong sales skills, commitment, and the financial ability to stay with it.

**People skills**—sales is a people business, plain and simple. Good salespeople have to be able to relate well with others, and at the same time, understand that it's not about them—the agents—it's about the customer. If a candidate is not able to relate well with you during two separate interviews, how well do you think that person will do in the field?

**Confidence** — a person's belief in him- or herself, and his or her ability to do something. Agents ask people to trust them with the largest single investment most will make in their lifetime.

**Enthusiasm**—an evident level of enjoyment in what one does is essential in sales.

**Tech-savvy skills**—technology plays an increasingly important role in real estate, and that role changes daily. It is an important tool that is essential in business today.

**Motivation/work ethic**—what is their motivation to succeed? How have they achieved success in the past? Every salesperson is only as good as his or her last month's numbers—the tough part is the commitment it takes to get there.

**Trainable**—are they trainable? Do they understand that dynamic training and practice that is aligned to today's market conditions, and to the consumer, are critical to their success?

**Coachable**—are they willing to take direction and have you hold them accountable to what they have told you they want (i.e., their goals and objectives)?

How do they view your role in their success? Do they understand that a skilled hands-on broker can make all the difference?

After you have assessed all of the above, ask your self:

*If I interviewed a well-qualified candidate today, what competitive advantages do I offer them?*

Does your answer show a true competitive differentiation, or do you look like your competitors? If there's no significant difference between your sign and the sign down the street, agents will make their decision on commission split. If you can show you have an effective program for their success, and a track record to support your claims you are positioned for strong recruiting results.

Now ask yourself, "Have I actually faced these issues, or am I imagining them?" It is interesting to note that many times these reflect what you believe, not issues you've actually encountered from a recruit.

## Social Media as a Recruiting Tool

Begin using Facebook and LinkedIn; you can expand from there into Twitter and blogs. Minimum of once weekly, post about the events, training, discussions, market research, etc. going on in your company. Postings should be around activities. Use video clips of your training or market stats discussions. Comment on your book club meetings. Ask questions. Ask for opinions and comments. (Reference Chapter 10 for weekly posting directives).

It takes time to build a "following" so keep it going – even if you think no one is listening.

*Recently I was working in a company and we were discussing the use of social media. The owner was surprised to learn that the top agent of another company had inquired about who I was and what I would discuss with the agents/management. (The owner had posted on Facebook that she and her agents were looking forward to my visit and what they would learn). It wasn't about me; it was about what the owner was doing to move the company forward – and someone was paying attention – unknown to her.*

To simplify your approach to postings, pick the same day of the week to update your business related postings. Use a casual photo on Facebook – which is consumer to consumer. Use a business photo on LinkedIn  - which is a business to business platform.

Start with these and build your presence, expanding to other outlets as they become relevant to the consumer or industry.

As you build your presence on Social Media, you'll want to track your results.

Try: *NutShellMail.com* or *ConstantContact.com/social media* for help in tracking.

## Database

*If you take the time to set up your database and follow-up system beforehand, you'll be able to get right to making your calls without spending valuable time "getting ready."*

**Database/follow-up system**—you can use any contact-management system or a "tickler" system. The key is to forward each lead to the next *date* that you intend to contact them, so that you will receive an alert/reminder and you don't forget. Consistency of follow up is critical to strong recruiting.

**Defining leads—cold, warm, and hot** —this is pretty straightforward, and I've outlined specifics.

A *cold lead* is a candidate who has no apparent reason or desire to join you at this point. Still, things change, and based on your research this is an agent that you'd like to hire if he or she wants to make a move. Follow-up once a month, and set the follow-up alert for every thirty days.

A *warm lead* shows some interest and seems curious during your calls. Follow up every couple of weeks; set follow-up alert for every two to three weeks.

A *hot* lead is motivated to make a move in the next thirty days. Follow-up a few times each week; set follow-up alert for two to three times a week. Don't worry about what you'll say – the urgency of the situation will give you plenty of dialogue.

Only one question remains: *"Who ya' gonna call?"*

## New versus Experienced Agents

### New Agents
Call around career nights. Call into neighborhoods where you'd like to see more signs. Call exam lists. Teach RE school/class. Advertise online. Use social media. **Use your website**. Network with other industries: insurance, advertising, high-end car sales. Consider people currently out of work. Develop several areas from which to recruit.

## Experienced Agents

Today's world requires you to research possible recruits before contacting them. No more relying on a purely social approach to recruiting; rather, you must use a strong lead-in that lets agents know that you know something about them, and that you're paying attention. It's a compliment to them, and it cuts to the chase—after all, they know why you're calling them. I highly recommend that you use Terra Datum's Broker Metrics, or similar software that interfaces with your MLS and provides you with information that used to take a lot of time to acquire. Follow them on Social Media – you can learn a lot.

**Research the following key questions**—What is their number of listings now? What is their DOM? What is their LT versus their LS? What is their YTD business versus the previous year? This kind of information will allow you to see strengths and weaknesses in possible recruits—look to your program, and you'll know how you can help them. Understand that it is your ability to offer business guidance to the recruit that matters most today. As for the rest of it, they've heard it all before.

Newer agents are a great source for finding recruits. Many of newer agents have not received the training, support, or direction promised to them, yet they remain motivated.

As our markets have slowed, there are more agents than ever who receive little or no support from their brokers. We have tendency to overestimate our competitors. Get on the phone! Connect with them on Social Media platforms.

**Sources for experienced agents**—at the first sales meeting of each month ask your agents the following: *"I'm looking to improve our market share, and I want to make it easier for all of you to list and sell—who do you know that might add something to the office?"* Explain what you want in/expect from an agent, as most believe that you are only interested in top producers.

**Co-broke agents**—those agents who've worked on a transaction with your company.

**Newer agents**—track the new agents you missed hiring; call them after one month—most don't get what the brokers who hired them promised to deliver.

It pays to keep in mind that you want someone who wants the program you provide—and who will add something to your company. Your research and your interviews will take you in the right direction.

## Calculate Number of Calls

### Number of Hires = Number of Calls

First, calculate the number of agent hires you'll need to achieve your desired increase in production/profit. Based on your planned production increase for this year, how many agents will you need to hire?

In calculating new hires, look at your track record: If you want to hire twelve new agents, how many will you have to hire to net twelve productive agents by year-end? In other words, if you hired eighteen, would you net twelve?

Second, to calculate experienced hires needed, if you do your homework and follow both recruiting interviews provided, the likelihood is that you will retain the number that you hire (i.e., if you hired twelve experienced agents, you'll have twelve experienced hires at year-end).

Third, factor in turnover. All businesses have it. Plan for it.

### Calculate the number of calls you'll need to make.

I use this formula: 80 x # agents/weeks/days= total # of calls.
20 contacts = 1appt.; 4appts. = 1 hire

That means that if you want twelve experienced agent hires, you must figure:
80 x 12 = 960 (contacts)
960 ÷ 40 (total weeks worked in a year) = 24 (contacts per week)
24 ÷ 4 (number of days you recruit each week) = 6 (contacts per day)

For every four contacts, you should net one appointment – an average based on new and experienced hiring.

Figure ten contacts per hour. In this example, schedule forty minutes a day for recruiting.

Attempts are not contacts. Talking to people counts as contacts.

Start your pipeline now. It is a process. Patience and persistence count.

Your primary opportunity to hire people in your pipeline will come as a result of one of the following:

- Change in the market and/or no direction/support from their broker
- Major event in the agent's personal life
- Production slump and/or no broker support
- Negative incident within the agent's current office/company
- Merger/acquisition
- Competing broker
- Unethical broker

## Know Your Competition

Compile info on your competition; list pros and cons. It is amazing what we don't know about our competition. Start now. Use any system that works for you, but be sure to list everything you know about at least six of your competitors. You'll add to this information as you recruit—their agents prove to be a big resource for additional information here. Refer to this information before calling/interviewing anyone working at these companies so that you can ask questions around the information you've acquired.

Broker Metrics or similar software can help here as well. I urge clients to use it to research entire offices, not just individual agents. You may find that an office could be at risk to close due to low production, and then you'll have an opportunity to build relationships with agents before that happens—this will help you avoid as appearing to be an "ambulance chaser."

## Research

"New" used to be a fairly simple and straightforward hire, but it has become more complicated. New agents are doing their homework and preparing a list of questions for you. Do not feel threatened by this; instead, be appreciative that they are serious enough to do this. Remember, good hires look for a good interview. The interview puts you in control and keeps things on your track.

When speaking with a potential new-agent hire before the actual interview, use the "Pre-Appointment Questions" —they'll save you a lot of time doing interviews with people who are not cut out for sales for some very basic reasons (i.e., cannot live on a commission income).

With potential experienced-agent hires, ask open-ended questions to get them talking about themselves. Your job is to listen.

**Be sure that you have done research on each experienced agent!** *Again, I highly recommend using Terra Datum's Broker Metrics.*

I have listed "categories" for experienced agents, along with a number of questions that will help you get your conversations moving forward. Select the questions that are relevant based on what you know about the agent you are contacting. Be conversational, but do not be an inquisitor; and again, concern yourself with listening and understanding their responses.

I have listed a number of questions to help you get started—match them with your research on the agent, and then just let the conversation unfold. Respond with what you offer that can solve the agents' challenges when appropriate.

**Newer Agent** *(agents with up to two years in RE)*

*How you are enjoying the real-estate business?*

*Is it what you expected?*

*Are you where you thought you'd be, given the amount of time you're investing?*

*How do you feel about the direction and support you're getting from your manager?*

*How often does your manager meet with you one-on-one to help you?*

*How do you feel about where you are so far this year?*

*What are your greatest challenges in conducting business?*

*What are you learning in this market?*

*What would help you most?*

*What are your goals and priorities this year? What actions are you taking to achieve them?*

*Do you work from a business plan?*

*How often does your manager meet with you to help you stay on track?*

*How do you think a new office could help your business?*

*Have you checked out our website – there's a lot of information that could be of interest to you. Connect with the agent on various social media.*

## Agent Referral/Co-Broke

*One of my agents, "Susie Smith," thinks highly of you and mentioned your professionalism when you worked together on . . . What do you believe you offer that sets you apart? (Listen for the response before continuing!) After Susie's recommendation, I did some research on your production this year and I was interested to find . . .*

*What do you think has contributed to your success?*

*Do you work from a business plan?*

*Are you on track to meet your goals and objectives this year?*

*Do you receive coaching from your manager? If yes, how has it helped? or Why not?*

*What do you think would help you most at this point?*

*What systems do you have in place to build your business?*

*How have you integrated statistics into your business?*

*What's your Social Media strategy? Are you integrating real estate? How?*

These are but a few questions that will get you started. You can use the interview questions even at this stage. Put the interview into a file with the agent's name on it and write down their responses. When you hold an actual interview, verify that your information is still correct. The agent will be impressed that you actually listened to what he or she said during the call.

## Agent Objections

How often do we hear the following, once we are on the phone? "I'm too busy." "I'm happy." "I'm not interested in moving." " I'd have to have a certain commission split before I'd consider a move." These are the most common. I call these *learned responses.* They have little to do with reality; rather, they are just common responses. (Think of these responses as similar to our response of "Just looking," when a salesperson in a store approaches us—regardless of whether we are there for a good reason.)

Learn to expect these responses and to treat them for what they are—objections and a normal part of the sales process. Keep in mind that, at the very least, they *are* talking to you!

I've listed a few counter-response suggestions:

If they are "busy"—and production is down—ask if they are experiencing an increase in their business, and if so, how do they account for it? If they are "busy"—and their production is up—ask about their systems and what support they receive to handle the increase.

If they are "happy"—and production is down—ask why. If they are "happy"—and business is improving—ask why it is improving and how they are handling this increase. What systems do they use? Do they have admin support?

If "they are not interested in moving"—and recently agents have added to this statement that *if they don't start making money where they are, they'll leave real estate altogether.* This presents an opportunity: Probe to learn if the agent will have to get "a real job" if they leave. If so, ask what kind of work they expect to find, given the current unemployment rate, and if they can find employment, what they expect to receive as a salary. Many have not thought all of this through, and so they do not realize that they have few options. Plus, most agents have no idea what it's like to work for a broker with a clear path for their success—and many doubt that such an environment actually exists. You and your program can change that.

If the agent "wants a high commission split"—ask how much income they want this year. What's the most important issue: split or income? High splits do not insure income level. Ask, "What do you want to earn this year? Which is more important to you, an 85 percent split or earning that amount?"

Over the years, these are the agent issues that I have heard most frequently:

"I do not know what to do in this market." "I get no broker direction and no support in coaching." "I don't receive relevant training." "I work too much/too hard, but I'm making less money." "I have too much admin work to do." "I have no life."

These are the most-common agent goals: more time off; more control of their time while working; taking their business to the next level; building a team or hiring an assistant.

Brokers make the mistake of assuming that agents only want to make more money—it's not about the split. We talk way too much, instead of listening to them, and most of the time, we sell too soon—and before we have learned what's important to the agent.

The majority of the time, you can solve the agent's problems and help them achieve their goals through business planning, coaching, a dynamic training program, and the right technology direction.

I have included recruiting "Recruiting Pre-Appointment Questions" and "Recruiting Interviews" for both new and experienced agents. If you are a multi-office company, all managers should use the same interviews, value package, etc. Consistency is critical.

Form follows.

# RECRUITING PRE-APPOINTMENT QUESTIONS

*These are the recruiting questions that you would ask a new agent in order to determine whether the candidate meets minimum company requirements for an interview. Italics are for your consideration.*

Are you considering a career in real estate as a full-time or part-time sales associate?
*Do you really want to hire a part-time salesperson? How will you train and coach this person? What are the real chances of his or her succeeding?*

Do you understand that real estate is commission paid—that means no salary or draw? Can you afford to live on a commission basis? If so, for how long?

Why real estate? What do you think a real-estate salesperson does all day? Have you thought about how you'll build your business? Do you use social media? What kind of presence do you have in the community?

*If you are satisfied with the responses, set the appointment. Make sure he or she knows how to get to your office. Request that he or she brings a résumé to the interview.*

## Recruiting Interviews

Qualified people are expecting a good interview process. They are taking your measure and deciding whether they are more or less likely to be successful working for you.

The interview allows you to maintain control and keeps you on your track.

Make a file for each agent that you interview. Write down the responses to your questions and keep your notes in each interviewee's file. How else will you remember the responses of every person you interview?

**Remember, this is a qualifying process, not a sales process.**

Conduct two interviews for each agent. Be sure to give the prospective agents the assignment at the end of the first interview. They're trying to get hired, so they are eager to please at this point. If the agents won't take direction now, what are the chances they will once you've hired them?

Before you interview, you must be clear about who you are and what you offer. Most brokers have a reactive response to their competition and believe that they must match their compensation offerings. If you are offering this program for the agents' success, you are not comparing apples to apples. A high split does not guarantee earnings. The right hire, a business plan, one-on-one coaching, dynamic training, and the necessary admin and tech support *will guarantee earnings.* If you don't believe it, how can you sell it?

*In the interview forms that follow, the first paragraph is your opening conversation with each candidate; the rest are the actual interview questions.*

# First and Second Recruiting Interviews – New Agents

## FIRST RECRUITING INTERVIEW – NEW AGENT

Name:                                          Date:

*"Let me begin by explaining the interview process we'll go through together: I'll take you through a fairly detailed interview that will help both of us make a mutual decision about your affiliation with us. After the first interview, I'll review your answers—and I hope you'll do the same—and then we'll meet for a second interview to cover any follow-up questions. At that point, I'll go over what it's like to work with us, including the tools we have in place for your success, as well as what we'll expect of you and what you can expect from me."*

Tell me about yourself.


What are your expectations for today's interview?


Are you employed currently? *If yes:* Tell me what you like most about your job responsibilities. *Whether yes or no:* What other jobs have you held?


Why do you believe that you are cut out for a job in real-estate sales? What do believe that you will bring to the company?


What do you think a real-estate salesperson does all day long?


Have you thought about how will you generate and build your business?

Tell me about your involvement in your community. How many people do you know who would be willing to refer business to you? Will you be willing to contact them? How?

How has the Internet impacted the real-estate business?

Do you own a laptop computer? Do you own a smart phone? How will you use technology in your business? What did you think of our online presence?

Tell me about the best boss you ever had. Why was he or she the best? Now tell me about the worst you ever had. Why was he or she the worst? How do you like to be supervised?

How would your best boss describe you? How would your worst boss describe you?

What are you looking for in a manager? What are you looking for in a company?

How much money do you intend to make in real estate your first year? What about in three years? What's the most money you've ever made in one year?

What does success mean to you? What does failure mean to you? Tell me about a past success and a past failure.

If your friends/coworkers were asked to describe you, what would they say? Have you ever had difficulties with a coworker? Why?

If you could change one thing about yourself, what would it be? How would you like to grow professionally? What about personally?

Can you think of a time you went "above and beyond" in your work? Are you proud of the work that you do?

What questions/concerns do you have for me?

How would you prefer that I contact you—phone, voice mail, or e-mail?

**If you are interested, let the candidate know!**
*At this point, set your next appointment if appropriate. Second appointment covers your expectations (i.e., business plan, minimum production standard, coaching program, training requirements, etc.). At the second interview, you will also revisit any questions/concerns you have from first interview.*

**Give the candidate an assignment.**
*Have the prospect read one book before your next interview (i.e., The New Rules of Marketing and PR). Also, have him or her put together an SOI list to bring to the second interview. Be specific about who to include in the SOI.*

# CANDIDATE ASSESSMENT – NEW AGENT

*Fill this out after the first interview to more accurately evaluate the candidate.*

Generational group:

Personality style:

Level of empathy:

Level of drive:

Coachable:

Trainable:

First impression:

Strengths:

Weaknesses:

Sense of humor:

Intelligence:

Tech savvy:


Rank them (ascending scale of 1–5) on the following:

Interpersonal skills     _____
Confidence     _____
Enthusiasm     _____
Experience     _____
Dependability     _____
Motivation     _____
Image/professionalism     _____
SOI     _____
Tech-savvy skills     _____

## SECOND RECRUITING INTERVIEW – NEW AGENT

*The follow-up interview begins with your asking any additional questions from the first interview—probe for additional information. Answer any questions the candidate might have for you.*

**Now is the time to sell your value program and show how each item is designed for the agent's success. Back up your claims with your company statistics.**

**If you want to hire this person, *lay out your expectations now.***

I require every agent in this office to:

- Own and use a smart phone and a laptop.
- Meet a minimum production standard.
- Learn to work from a business plan, which I will provide and teach you how to use.
- Complete the new-agent training program, as scheduled.
- Learn to build and generate business using the SOI system and Social Media.
- Complete the _____ designation within your first year.
- Receive weekly coaching one-on-one with me in order to obtain the support needed to reach your desired goals and objectives.
- Attend sales meetings and other additional training, as offered.*
- Learn the Company Listing Presentation.
- Learn the Company Buyer Presentation.

*\*At this point, you must stress that perfecting professional skills is an ongoing process for everyone in your company. **Emphasize professional mastery!***

Fill out the SOI Annual Plan. Fill out the Goals Worksheet (in order to fulfill minimum production standard or one transaction per month). Show the candidate what he or she will need to do, Monday through Friday, in order to work for you. Is he or she willing to fulfill your expectations? If so, offer the job. Explain your commission schedule.

**Communicate your belief in the candidate's ability to be a successful real-estate agent.**

**Oversee a smooth transition over the first thirty days. Schedule each of them for weekly coaching meetings. Make sure you deliver everything you promised during the interviews. Kept promises build trust and credibility and retention.**

# First and Second Recruiting Interviews – Experienced Agents

## FIRST RECRUITING INTERVIEW – EXPERIENCED AGENT

*For experienced agents, the purpose of the first recruiting interview is for you introduce the importance of your fully understanding the agent's business, goals, and objectives, and finally, whether or not you mutually feel that you should go forward together.*

Name:                                               Date:

How long have you worked with _____?

Have you ever worked for anyone else? *If yes:* Who? Why did you leave?

What did you do before real estate?

What do you enjoy most about RE? What do you enjoy least? If you could change one thing about our industry, what would it be?

What do you think the most significant changes in our business during the last two years have been? How have you changed the way you conduct business as a result?

How do you use technology in your business? How have you used your website/webpage to generate business? What results do you track? Do you use social media? What do you think about our online presence?

How do you feel about what you've accomplished this year? Is it in line with your goals and priorities? *If no:* What actions will you take?

Did you reach your goals last year? What do you think contributed to your reaching—or missing—your goals? What are you learning in today's market?

Do you work from a business plan? How do you stay on track? What would help you most at this point?

How often does your manager meet with you to review your priorities and help you stay on track? How do you think a new company will benefit you? What will you add to the company?

What is your average rate of commission per side of closed business? What is your average DOM for your current listing inventory? What is your LS versus LT? Do you use absorption-rate pricing analysis?

Do you track where your business comes from? How often do you work your SOI? What system do you use to track your SOI contacts? What is the generational breakdown of your client base? How have you adapted to their needs and expectations?

What do you do currently to market yourself? What do you spend annually on self-promotion?

How does the office administrative staff support you? What would help you administratively to save time? What company tools do you use currently?

How many hours/days a week do you work currently? Do you do a good job of balancing your personal and professional life?

What are your biggest challenges/frustrations in your work?

Describe the perfect real-estate office. How will a new office impact your ability to succeed?

What mortgage and closing companies do you use? What have they done differently to keep your business? What liquidity issues have you faced?

If asked to describe you, what would your clients/coworkers say?

What training classes have you attended in the last year? Did you implement anything as a result?

If you could change one thing about yourself, what would it be? How would you like to grow professionally? What about personally?

Can you think of a time you went "above and beyond" in your work? Are you proud of the work that you do?

What concerns do you have about making a move?

What questions do you have for me?

How would you prefer that I contact you—phone, voice mail, or e-mail?

*If you are interested at this point, communicate that to the candidate! Remember, this is an experienced agent, so your expression of interest is critical.*
*If appropriate, set a second appointment. Stress that you would like to review the interview questions and make sure you a thorough understanding of his or her issues and objectives.*

**Give the candidate an assignment.**
*Ask the agent to read the "New Rules of Marketing and PR" (By David Meerman Scott) .*

# CANDIDATE ASSESSMENT

*Use this form to clearly evaluate the candidate after the first interview.*

Generational group:

Personality style:

Level of empathy:

Level of drive:

Coachability:

Trainability:

Intelligence:

Sense of humor:

*When answering the following questions, keep in mind that this is an **experienced** agent!*

What are the candidate's priorities?

What are the candidate's concerns?

What are the candidate's weaknesses And strengths?

How will joining your office/company benefit him or her? How will it benefit you?

What concerns do you have at this point?

## SECOND RECRUITING INTERVIEW – EXPERIENCED AGENT

Probe for additional information based on the first interview. If you have doubts, clearly communicate your expectations—and show how your company will support the agent through business planning, one-on-one coaching, dynamic training, and admin and tech support. Use the SOI Annual Plan and the Goals Worksheet.

If this is an agent who will definitely add something to your company, go through each one of his or her issues and objectives, and then show how what you offer in your company will resolve these.

Explain what the agent can expect from you. This should include the following: monthly market statistics, business planning, one-on-one coaching, dynamic training, admin and tech support, a personal marketing strategy (SOI), company presentations, and the absorption-rate analysis.

Fill out the SOI Annual Plan and Goals Worksheet. Is the agent willing to do the work?

If so, *now is the time to cover your expectations!* Let me repeat that: not after hiring, **now!**

I require every agent who works in this office to:

- Own and use a smart phone and a laptop.
- Prepare and use a business plan.
- Attend sales meetings.
- Attend training programs.
- Learn presentations.
- Participate in coaching.

Add anything you like to the above list. Ask if you have left any of the candidate's concerns unanswered.

Then ask: *Have you thought about how to handle your resignation? What will you say to your broker when you leave?*

Prepare him or her for the exit interview with the current broker. This will include the likelihood of his or her being offered a higher split to stay—will this resolve the candidate's issues/objectives?

Counsel the candidate about what to say, noting that this is a common concern for agents making a move. In the end, it is a business decision. If the candidate has strong concerns about the current broker's response, advise him or her to move out the night before (he or she can move right in to your office). Suggest that he or she meet with the current broker early in the morning on the following day to resign. Stress that this meeting should be brief, and then make sure the transition to your office is as smooth as possible. If all else fails, he or she can make a night move, and you can inform the current broker the next day.

The first thirty days after hiring are the most important! You must oversee a smooth transition—and deliver what you promised during the interviews. Remember, kept promises build trust and credibility. Make sure you have done a business plan with this hire, and also that you have put him or her into your coaching schedule. This hire will "take your measure" during this time, just as you will take his or hers. Again, this is the time when you build trust and credibility for future retention—on both your parts.

## Recruiting Value Package

Today, this can be showcased best on **your website**. This allows an agent to browse through it when they have an interest or maybe something has sparked their curiosity.

**What to post?**

Understanding first, that transparency is a good thing –

Post your monthly company statistics: DOM; %LS; Actual SP% vs. Original LP
Use video clips from your training classes.
Video any special training offering with an outside speaker
Post your Agent Business Plan and Mid Review
Post your Listing Presentation Checklist
Post your Buyer Presentation Checklist
Post your Agent Coaching Form
Post your monthly training schedule
Use a video from a company social event

You get the idea.

**When using a hard copy of your value package...**

Tailor this to the recruit! I like a pocket folio with sections for each category—that way, if you have to make changes, you only need to reprint one section. Examples of section topics include the following: business development (planning and coaching); training (new and experienced); admin support (coordinators, etc.); technology package; management; staff; etc. **DVDs** and online access to documents are valuable as well, and these appeal to the younger agent. Make sure the packet contains things that interest the agent. Differentiate. If the agent is joining because of business planning and coaching, make sure the packet has a copy of your latest agent business plan and a copy of the agent coaching form. **Do not include your commission schedule until you are ready to hire!** *An agent who joins you for commission will leave you for commission.*

## Exit Interview
**Prepare the candidate for leaving his or her current office.**
Coach his or her resignation. Most are very intimidated at the thought of it. Use role -play to take the agent through the conversation with the current broker. Let the agent know to

expect an offer of a higher commission split—what else does the broker know to do? Will the higher split resolve the candidate's issues? Will anything else?

*It is important for you to be very clear as to why this candidate wants to join your office. If you aren't clear at this point, don't kid yourself—they're not joining.*

## First Thirty Days

The first thirty days in your company are critical to the agents you hire—whether new or experienced. Make sure you have good systems and organization for orientation into your company and your procedures. Delegate most of this to your staff.

Schedule an appointment during the agent's first week in order to develop a business plan and set up a coaching program with you. Failure to do this can damage your credibility with these agents forever—once again, the agent was promised things that are not delivered.

Another benefit to doing all this is the possibility of other agents from the new hire's former company calling to ask how he or she "likes it" in your office. You want the newly recruited agent to be your advocate.

## Mergers and Acquisitions

One of the most attractive ways to grow a company today is to look for other companies that are ripe for a merger or an acquisition (M/A). This can be a means to a growth spurt if you properly analyze both company and culture before making the leap.

If your goal is to expand geographically, the same analysis applies. Also consider who will run the operation and make sure they are onboard with your program. You running two offices at once usually means they both suffer.

First, ask yourself if there are more gains to be made by recruiting the agents who are worth hiring—rather than taking on a larger group whose aggregate might not add up to much. In other words, skip the M/A, and instead, just recruit those who will add something to your company.

### Financial Analysis

M/A numbers must make a lot of sense here, and I have included the industry-accepted "formula" for determining value.

> Review the **last three years**, including:
> - profit-and-loss (P&L) statements
> - agent rosters (i.e., are agents leaving?)
> - production summaries by agent (i.e., growing or losing production)
> - Consider the effects of any production done by current management/ownership:
> - actual agent commission splits and perks
> - overall, is this company worth the effort and disruption that the M/A would entail? Will this add to your bottom line?

## Other Key Considerations

Other significant issues with mergers/acquisitions do exist. Although often overlooked, these issues make all the difference regarding whether—or not—the M/A will be successful, or even worth your time to consider.

Compare company/office cultures—the people matter. Consider programs and policies, ethics, commission splits, training expectations, current management style, and staff services. *Do not operate under the impression that you can merge people when these differences exist—or that it won't be painfully obvious to all concerned if you try to do so.* Real estate has few secrets—if you allow higher splits to coexist with your current schedule, you are asking for trouble. If your existing agents believe that you have lowered your standards to bring on new people, you stand to lose the agents you want to retain. Individually interview each agent in the company you are considering for M/A—use the recruiting interview—and then make the decision to hire, or not hire, accordingly.

> *I have a client who runs a successful company on the West Coast. His franchise approached him about merging with a nearby office that was in trouble. Though I counseled otherwise, he went ahead with the merger, wasting valuable time and money on it, only to have the owner of the other company unravel it all the night before—thus destroying any chances of the merger's success.*

*Moral: It may look better for the franchise to show that offices are merging, rather than closing, but is it better for you? Bigger isn't necessarily better—sometimes bigger is just bigger. My client took his eye off of his company for an extended period of time—for nothing.*

## Valuation

Not much money is changing hands today; most of the owners of the companies to be merged are happy to walk away from the monthly debt. Be careful that you do not incur any of their expenses (leases, etc.) unwittingly.

I've included an industry-recognized form for computing value.

Form follows.

# RESIDENTIAL REAL-ESTATE COMPANY VALUATION –
# INCOME APPROACH

INCOME

Income before taxes                                    $_____
+
Depreciation                                           $_____
+
Amortization                                           $_____
+
Interest expenses                                      $_____
+
Owner compensation                                     $_____
+
Owner benefits                                         $_____
+
Nonrecurring expenses                                  $_____

Equals total income items                              $_____

CHARGE BACKS TO INCOME

Comparable cost of management                          $_____
-
Nonrecurring expenses                                  $_____
-
Owner contribution to company revenue                  $_____
-
Interest or dividend income                            $_____

Equals charge backs against income                     $_____

Total income items                                     $_____

- Less total charge backs                              $_____

Equals EBITDA or
Income valuation                                       $_____

Income                                                 $_____
Times the multiple            X_____
Equals total value                                     $_____

# 7

# Company Training Program

This is the area behind which the real-estate industry should be putting its collective muscle. Any strategy for long-term growth and profit must align with the needs and wants of the consumer. We must get better at what we do! All of us must improve the delivery of our services, and multi-office companies must strive for consistency within all offices.

Ultimately, training programs and requirements will reflect that which a company believes about the importance of customer service. Your ability to teach agents to build and grow their business begins in your training program. Strong training strengthens recruiting and retention. Management must roll up their sleeves, demonstrate their expertise, and become an integral part of every agent's business. If this is not evident and credible to your agents, why should they work with you?

I still hear directives, such as "Our goal is to increase our market share by 20 percent this year." Or, "If you don't produce more, you're gone." This is the stuff failure is made of—anybody can talk. But just talking has nothing to do with leadership and skilled management. Where is the how? Where is the concerted effort directed toward the increases?

The philosophy to "train as if your business depends on it" is one on which the real-estate industry should spend time.

## New-Agent Training

New-agent training should be 50 percent technical skills (finance, stats, technology, legal, agency, disclosures, etc.) and 50 percent sales skills (presentations, objection handling, generating business, pricing etc.).

Use reality dialogues and case studies extensively in order to demonstrate mastery. If an agent can't dialogue effectively in front of you, the likelihood that he or she will use the training with the consumer is slim to none. Flying by the seat of the pants is no way to do business in today's world—and we have gotten by with it for far too long. Remember, today's real-estate industry is consumer oriented.

I've provided a sample list of topics—add others based on your market conditions.

I strongly urge management to set mandatory training-program requirements. No agent works in the field until he or she can demonstrate successful completion of the company training program. Tell your agents what you expect from the very beginning (i.e., during the recruiting interviews).

> *I once worked with a company whose training director offered no training until the agent began working on a transaction. She was surprised to learn that I expected agents to complete a full training program before brokers "unleashed" those agents on an unsuspecting consumer. She is no longer the training director.*

Below is a list of topics that will help you start/improve your company training program.

## Company Training Topics

### Orientation to Office/Company

Review workstation setup (desk assignment, e-mail, voice mail, website, paperwork, tour of office, ancillary services, etc.).

Review information on Board of Realtors: Fair Housing; orientation; MLS training.

*You can delegate many of the these training items to a staff member.*

Have a checklist for the new agent to work with; it should include a column next to each topic where he or she can notate completion dates.

### Building a Business
SOI System
SOI Annual Plan
Effective Social Media
Goals Worksheet
Working from a Business Plan (M–F)
Lead Mastery (phone, web, OH, etc.)
Lead Follow-up System
Time Management

**Listing Presentation**
Research and Preparation
Pre-Appointment Questions
Listing Presentation
Absorption-Rate Analysis
Future Price Reductions
Backup Mortgage Approval
Seller Objections/Questions
Listing Documents
Listing Package
Seller's Net Sheet
Open Houses
Contract Presentation
Negotiating the Offer
Contract to Closing
Settlement Issues
Seller Customer Service – Communication
Generational Issues

**Buyer Presentation**
Market Statistics
Pre-Appointment Questions
Financial Approval
Buyer Interview
Agency Overview
Showing Property
Absorption-Rate Pricing
Backup Mortgage Approval
Writing the Offer
Presenting the Offer
Negotiating the Offer
Contract to Closing
Preferred Vendors
Settlement Issues
Customer Service Follow-up
Generational Issues

**Technical Classes**
Agency
Listing Agreement
Sales Contract/Contingencies/Addenda
Mandatory Disclosures
Technology
Financing (*use your LO*)

Construction
Settlement/Escrow
Internet/Company Website/Social Media
Agent Webpage/Website
Intranet
MLS

*Add to the classes listed above any other topics that your state and/or local jurisdictions require.*

## Experienced-Agent Training

Effective training for experienced agents is almost nonexistent, and most who seek it out, go outside the company to get it. Many brokers are intimidated by experienced, productive agents; and so they tend to leave them alone. Most of these agents pulled themselves up by their initiative, and they don't know as much as we give them credit for. We are mistaken if we believe that they will admit to this fact—most carefully hide it. Their competitive stats can reveal a lot.

Training programs for experienced agents should be 25 percent technical skills and 75 percent sales skills. The training content remains the same; the classes change based on the experience and dialogue from the participants. Case studies and dialogues are critical for improvement at this level in order to determine where their strengths and weakness lie.

These will measure the agent's comprehension of the subject matter—and whether it will be applied in the marketplace. Most work within their comfort zone, and if they are not comfortable with something, it's unlikely they'll risk making a fool of themselves in front of others. Hence, nothing changes for consumer or agent or company.

### Attendance

Many brokers complain that experienced agents won't attend training classes. If this is true for you, try the following steps. First, make sure that what you're offering has value under current market conditions. Next, appeal to the experienced agents' egos by requiring a minimum level of production in order to attend. Finally, allow the classes to be interactive and make sure to address generational differences.

Brokers often overlook where their "power" is. It is in their one-on-one interactions with the agents, plain and simple. Find time to target each agent, remind them of the classes, and let them know you expect them to attend as the class will help them with a current "need".

Don't be overly concerned that each class has to be new and exciting. Repetition is necessary. **Practice is vital**. Work on the basics. The exciting part comes when they "get it"! For most of them, it takes a while before it "clicks"—so stay with a topic until agents are able to dialogue comfortably. They may understand and agree with the instruction intellectually; however, that's still a long way from being able to deliver it effectively with a consumer. *Comprehension and confidence must accompany delivery of the subject* *matter. It takes practice.* If they are unable to be convincing in practice, how will they ever earn the trust with today's mistrustful consumer?

**Attendance is mandatory for all new agents—no exceptions and no excuses!**

I recommend that you take attendance and keep a record of all training classes for reference and accountability purposes.

I am including some of my training materials. These are not all-inclusive.

## Sphere of Influence (SOI)

### SOI Program for Business Generation – the first step

What directive do we have in place to teach agents how to build and generate business? Is it in line with today's consumer? Or do we tell them "any old thing"—a little of this and a little of that—just to get them to act busy. The consumer has long preferred working with and through people they know. Today's' younger consumer lives this approach.

If a company does not offer a specific program to build and grow business – why would a new or an experienced agent work with them?

The SOI system is based on a contact of every thirty days, varying amongst phone, e-mail, mail, in person and social media—and each contact must deliver something of value to that SOI member. I recommend monthly market statistics and JLJS (just listed/just sold), which show the consumer that the agent understands the market and is getting results.

The makeup of SOI should include past clients; friends and close neighbors; family; coworkers/contacts from previous careers; people agents know through family, clubs, and organizations.

Develop a system for tracking monthly contacts. Use any contact-management system that works—a laptop, or if preferred, a three-ring binder with one contact per page and numeric dividers (1–31) for the days of the month. Similar to using a "tickler" system, set alerts on the laptop to contact every thirty days; or, if using the binder, just refer to the day's date as a reminder of who to contact.

*[Forms for using SOI follow.]*

## SOI PERSONAL MARKETING SYSTEM

*Consider generational preferences when choosing the most effective way to work your SOI:*

- Phone – quarterly

- In person – once a year

- E-mail – no spam! Include social media strategy

- Mailing – JLJS postcards and market stats are the most effective mailings

*It's not about asking for something. It's about communication and sharing items of interest. It's about the consumer , **not** the agent. It's about building an ongoing relationship with your SOI—creating customers for life.*

Below is a list of reasons to contact SOI throughout the year. Add to this list based on what's going on in your market and community.

- In January, mail them a copy of their HUD 1 closing statement—they'll need it for the IRS. Give them a call and let them know you are sending it and why.

- **New Agents:** After sending announcements, call and let them know you have completed your training program. Show enthusiasm for your new career. Be sure to send JLJS to your SOI, as they will need to see you are doing business. Ask for e-mail addresses to send market stats.

- Call and update your database. Do you have e-mail addresses? Social Media?

- E-mail links to real-estate/market articles they might find interesting.

- Is it possible that their mortgages are in jeopardy? When do they adjust? Offer to have a lender offer possible refinance alternatives.

- If property values in your market area have appreciated/depreciated, call and give them a general percentage increase/decrease for their area. Remind them to update their homeowner's insurance so that they have full coverage.

- Do an absorption-rate analysis on the town, county, etc., and send out info.

- Email "Monthly Market Stats".

- Reference the "clue report" in order to alert them of claims that trigger a nonrenewal from their insurance companies.

- Have they considered real estate as an investment?

- Update them with any market news that could homeowners.

- Call with information on upcoming social events: festivals, parades, etc. Inquire as to whether they'll attend and indicate that you hope to see them. This is a particularly good one if they're new to the area or live outside the area.

- Movie tickets—buy a dozen tickets to the latest family blockbuster. Call and offer "tickets you can't use" to your SOI. Keep calling until you use up what you purchased. For the takers, put the tickets in an envelope with their name on it and your best wishes to "Enjoy the Show"—have them pick up the tickets at the front desk. They will love that you thought of them, even if they can't use the tickets.

- Mail or email JLJS postcards to your SOI—they need to see that you are conducting business. Always print on the bottom of the card: **"If you happen to know of anyone who's thinking of buying or selling this year, I'd love the opportunity to help."**

- Mail cards at Thanksgiving—it's great to feel appreciated!

- In person—buy personalized company scratch pads/calendars. The month you plan to "drop by," write on the top sheet: "Sorry I missed you . . . talk to you soon!" Make sure you sign the note. Few are ever at home, and they'll call you because you came by. Calendars work well for in person, too.

- **Reward your SOI!** If you get a referral, always send a small gift. It rewards the behavior that you want to see continue—even if the referral doesn't end up buying or selling.

Important! At the end of each contact say: *"Susie, if you and Jim come across anyone who's thinking of buying and selling, let me know. I'll be in touch again next month."*

I've also included the SOI Annual Report, which is a plan that agents can use to plot out **how** they will work their SOI every month. It is not necessary for agents to be specific, but rather just to note whether the contact will be a "call," "e-mail," "snail mail," or "in person." Include social-media strategy.

Post the page in plain sight and refer to it each month to guide their efforts, thus ensuring that their approaches remain varied. Include social media as a way to increase communication with SOI.

Watch for older agents who want to rely on mailings and younger agents who rely solely on e-mail or social media. Every agent's approach must be varied in order for them each to build the necessary relationships for effective real-estate professionals.

## SOI MONTHLY MARKETING PLAN

*Lay out your plan to network your SOI in 2011 (i.e., in person; telephone contact; e-mail; postcard, social media).*

January _____

February _____

March _____

April _____

May _____

June _____

July _____

August _____

September _____

October _____

November _____

December _____

Make sure to update your SOI database to include the following: address, phone number, work number, cell number, and e-mail address. Have you included your SOI in your social-media communications?

When you contact, be sure to close with: "If you happen to hear of anyone who might be thinking of buying or selling this year, I'd love the opportunity to help. If I don't hear from you, I'll be in touch again next month."

## Lead Mastery

Companies spend a lot of money generating business only to have the agent "drop the ball." Estimates of this are staggering. Teach an agent what to say—and what questions to ask—in order to demonstrate value to the consumer. **Throwing consumers into our cars "until they buy or die" is not an answer!**

Appropriate questions give us credibility and allow consumers to view agents as truly interested in them, the consumers, rather than only being interested in making the sale. The old sales adage quoted above developed for a reason. But remember, it no longer works—especially not in today's world.

You also need to teach agents a system for consistent follow-up and follow-through—the back of a cocktail napkin or yellow sticky notes won't get the job done.

### Lead-Mastery Dialogues

Teach agents to ask questions. This demonstrates concern, interest, and competence, and it also allows agents to gain valuable information so that they can better work with the consumers. Consider this all a part of the qualifying process and a necessity for doing our jobs effectively.

No matter how the lead originates, ask questions to determine the consumers' needs. Here are examples of **open-ended** questions:

"Thank you for inquiring. Let me get that information for you."

"**What** about the information appealed to you?"
 are you looking for in your new home?"
 is your time frame for making a move?"
 kind of home do you currently live in?"
 amenities are you looking for in your new home/neighborhood?"

"**Who** got the job transfer?"
 will make the buying decision?"
 do you know in the area?"
 else will be moving with you?"
 else will you interview to be your agent?"

**"Why** are you calling on this particular house?"

do you need four bedrooms?"

are you moving?"

will you rent rather than buy?"

**"When** do you plan to move?"

will you be ready to buy?"

does your new job start?"

can we get together to discuss your new home?"

**"Where** will you be working?"

have you looked for homes so far?"

would you prefer to be?"

**"How** will you pay for your new home?"

will you decide on a neighborhood?"

will you choose the agent you work with?"

many children do you have?"

long have you lived in your current home?"

close do you want to be to work?"

**"Will** you consider other towns/home styles?"

you move alone?"

you need to sell before you buy?"

anyone assist you with the purchase?"

schools be a consideration for you?"

public transportation be important?"

you have any special needs?"

you need to secure a mortgage?"

"We have several homes that might meet your needs. When can we get together to discuss how I can help you? Does Friday work or is Saturday better?"

[**Note:** Thanks to a former client, Dennis Bruce, Long and Foster for contributing the above scripts.]

### Internet Leads

Because most of Internet leads are doing research and may be months away from a buying/selling decision, you will need to keep them in a leads-management system with monthly follow-up (as already discussed). **Ask** *the following question, and then let* **them tell you** *what they want.*

**Internet response:** "Based on where you are in your search, what information can I send you that would help you most at this point?"

**Do biweekly follow-up**: First, e-mail top the portion of the "Monthly Market Stats" form; second, e-mail the percentage of distressed sales in your market. This is information that the consumer wants. Two e-mails; same format. The statistics change each month, and that keeps the consumer up-to-date. Keep it simple.

## Company Listing Presentation

Strong presentations persuade the consumer. You must base this persuasion on a careful analysis of market statistics, and use a logical process. Forget puffery. Forget opinions. Just the facts. Use statistics to back up market conditions, liquidity issues, your marketing proposal and your pricing proposal.

Consumers expect a professional presentation that qualifies the seller; explains options as the representation consumers can receive in the sale; gives a statistical overview of current market conditions; contains a marketing proposal and an absorption-rate pricing analysis; and covers the administrative aspects of the sale, as well as what the seller can expect from the agent in terms of follow-up and follow-through (complete with a written weekly report).

I have prepared a presentation checklist that includes the major topics every professional presentation should cover. Add other topics relative to your market conditions and known customer preferences.

*[Form follows.]*

# LISTING PRESENTATION CHECKLIST

o   Pre-Appointment Questions
o   Appointment to Preview
    *Preview and offer needed repair/maintenance service vendors, if appropriate.*
o   Listing Appointment/Presentation
o   Overview of Current Market/Finance Conditions
    *Use/cite stats here.*
o   Client Representation
    *Explain the options.*
o   Marketing Proposal – use SOB and Generational stats to justify
o   Lead Capture/Management System
    *Demonstrate on your laptop how this system works.*
o   Pricing – CMA vs. Absorption-Rate Analysis
    *Explain that pricing is reanalyzed every thirty days.*
o   Absorption-Rate Analysis – On All Contingent Offers
o   Backup Mortgage Approval
o   Price Reductions
    *Lay out format for future price reductions based on market.*
o   Service Vendors
    *Offer recommendations if not done previously.*
o   Offer Home Warranty
o   Documents/Disclosures
o   Listing Agreement
    *Have signed and provide copies for seller.*
o   Seller Net Sheet
o   Showing Instructions/Lockbox/Signage
o   Administrative Details
    *This should include online transaction management.*
o   Seller Packet
    *Leave this with them **only** when they sign agreement.*
o   Seller Follow-up/Follow-thru
    *Set this up to be done on a regular basis (i.e., follow-up every Monday evening). Lay out what you will go over with them (i.e., showing feedback, market activity, and marketing efforts of the past week). E-mail the absorption-rate report monthly for discussion.*
o   Negotiation of Offer
    *Remember who you represent. Use absorption-rate analysis to evaluate any contingent offer.*
o   Home Inspection Negotiation and Re-negotiation of contract
o   Transaction Management/Contract-to-Closing Guide
    *Stay in touch on a regular basis. Explain the process.*
o   Offers of additional services:
    *Home maintenance; home cleaning services; moving company, etc. Offer to show it on the HUD 1 (POC) so that it will detail on their closing statement, and they will have a record for IRS purposes.*
o   Client Follow-up Call
    *Make this call thirty days after closing the sale.*

## Company Buyer Presentation

The buyer is entitled to the same expectation of a professional presentation as the seller is. Buyers want a persuasive presentation, including more time spent up front finding out what's important to them; an overview of current market conditions (using stats) and how those conditions affect their ability to buy, as well as their options for the representation they will receive in the sale; and an absorption-rate pricing analysis on any property of interest to confirm that they are making the right pricing decision. The last thing a buyer in this market wants is to pay too much for a property. Buyers also expect to have their agent personally present their offer. Make sure the agent meets this expectation, which is essential if the agent is working as a "Buyer's Agent." Backup mortgage approval also helps to ensure that when buyers find their house, they can actually close the transaction—liquidity and appraisal issues abound.

> *On a subsequent visit to a company where I had taught their agents "The Buyer Presentation," one of their top agents spoke up to tell me how much he appreciated having one. He explained that he'd met an agent form another company at one of his listings (seller preference) and witnessed the agent meeting the buyer at the property and having the buyer sign a "form" on the hood of his car before going into the property. The other agent explained that he'd just met the buyer and had to get him to sign the agency disclosure form. The listing agent said it was then that he realized the difference in what he offered a consumer, as opposed to what he had just witnessed. His final comment was: "That's just not good enough for our company or our clients."*

*[Form follows.]*

# BUYER PRESENTATION CHECKLIST

## Via Telephone
- Agent Introduction
- Buyer Pre Appointment Questions
- Begin Loan Approval/Backup *(have LO call buyer)*
- Make initial buyer appointment *(at the office)*
- Call back or e-mail to confirm appointment *(give directions to office)*

## Initial Appointment
- Buyer Presentation Overview *(counsel the process and market/finance conditions—use stats)*
- Absorption-Rate Pricing *(counseling to position offer)*
- Buyer-Needs Analysis
- Present Agency Offerings/Options *(paraphrase for your state)*
- Final Loan Approval
- MLS Search *(while buyer is meeting with LO)*
- Offer of Representation
- Discuss Showings—neighborhoods versus properties *(saves time; show neighborhoods first, and then narrow down to properties, as appropriate)*

## After Showing Several Properties
- Re-evaluate *(if necessary).*

*After showing six to eight houses, sit down with the buyer and say: "I am concerned that I am not finding you what you're looking for; have I missed something, or have your priorities changed?"*

## Final Steps
- Write Offer
- Present Offer *(negotiate using absorption-rate pricing analysis)*
- Review Contract-to-Closing Events *(include home inspection renegotiation; in-depth HOA inquiry)*
- Online Transaction Management
- Contract-to-Closing Guide
- Follow-up *(at least weekly)*
- Customer Follow-up Call *(one month after closing)*

## Offer Additional Services
- Moving Company Referral
- Cleaning Service Referral
- Utilities Hookup Reminder
- Home-Services Contractor Referrals
- Home Warranty

# Absorption-Rate Analysis

How can we use a narrow comparative market analysis (CMA) to determine value in today's market? It's no wonder so much resale inventory is still overpriced and unsold! The absorption-rate analysis, in contrast, is an inventory-based approach to pricing, and it works in any and all market conditions. It is based on comparing similar properties in similar areas that the buyer might consider today.

Another great benefit is that the consumer actually understands this approach to pricing, as opposed to the outdated CMA approach, which does not illustrate the scope of competition in a market.

The bottom line is this: If we cannot advise the consumer on effective pricing, how can we do our job? What value do we provide for the fee they pay us?

In order to do a thorough analysis and be able to explain and defend their advice, agents must research the information that follows.

*The most important piece, so often overlooked, is to **think like today's buyer – most are more concerned with the best value, rather than an exact match of their expectations for the house.***

## Absorption Rate Analysis Preparation

**Pick the Areas**
- May not be just a sub area.
- Base it on *all* homes a buyer would look at and consider.

**How to Build Current Absorption Rate**
- Know the total number of listings pending.
- Know the average DOM.
- Know the total number of active listings
- Know the active listings' DOM.
- Know the number of listings currently expired/canceled
- Know the "price ranges" currently selling.
- Do a broad CMA for competition on market only.

**Do the Math**
- Pending Listings _____ + _____ Sold Listings = _____ Total Sold. *(Count properties once.)*
- _____ Total Sold / 2 Months = _____ Homes That Sell per Month in Your Price Range and Geographic Area. *(Based on the number of months supplied, determine where the property should be priced.)*

**Understand What the Market Tells You**

o   If the property is being shown and you have no offers: Buyers are finding better value elsewhere.

o   If a property is not being shown, agents are not finding enough value to show it to their clients.

**Be aware that both issues can be resolved with proper pricing!**

Simply put, *the point of taking a listing is to **sell it***—that's the job the seller hired you to do.

I have included "The Absorption-Rate Report" form. Use this form to illustrate to the consumer how you did your analysis. Written reports add credibility to your presentations and demonstrate that you "did the work" in order to arrive at your conclusion.

Remember, you prepare this analysis for both the seller *and* the buyer. Do not underestimate the importance of their need to fully understand the position of the property in relation to other inventory. Suffice it to say that this service builds credibility and consumer loyalty.

*[Form follows.]*

# ABSORPTION-RATE REPORT

*Go through this form step-by-step with consumers until they understand it. Repeat the analysis with each listing every thirty days.*

Date of report _____

Property address _____

Geographic areas studied for this analysis:

_____ _____

_____ _____

Price range studied for this analysis: _____

Total number active listings studied _____

Number of Listings Pending _____ + Number of Listings Sold _____ = Total Sold Listings _____

Total Sold Listings _____ / Number of Months Studied (2) = _____ Average Sales per Month

Total Active Listings _____ / Number of Average Sales per Month _____ = _____ Months of Inventory in Price Range and Geographic Areas Studied

## Reality Dialogues

You can also think of these as role-play classes. Regardless of what you call them, reality dialogues allow agents to demonstrate that they understand what you have taught them during training/coaching, because they show whether—or not—agents can effectively communicate information to consumers. Consider this practice an essential measurement of the agent's retained learning and ability to effectively use that with the consumer.

Reality dialogues teach agents how to respond competently and confidently—a communication style that is essential to their establishing consumers' trust.

**Practice, Practice, Practice!** Management and agents alike **_must practice_** until they have achieved mastery of the subject matter. Again, this is essential. The consumer deserves nothing less.

_[Class guidelines follow. Hold weekly classes, at minimum. Daily is optimal.]_

### Reality-Dialogue Classes

Hold reality-dialogue/role-play classes at least once a week. Each class should last at least an hour.

Topics can range from any or all of the following: Listing/Buyer Presentations; Lead-Mastery Questions; Working SOI, etc. Classes can also cover objections/issues agents currently face in the marketplace.

In classes that cover the presentations, take each section (use the checklist to define sections) and have two agents role play the buyer/seller/agent dialogues. _Stay with each section until agents are comfortable with the questions—they must begin to sound like they are having a natural conversation, rather than reading a script._ If they never get comfortable with the material, the chances of their actually using it are slim to none.

"Handling Objections" is a great class topic. Always cover the difference between an _objection_ and a _condition_. An _objection_ is a question/issue that remains unanswered in a client's mind. A _condition_ is something you can do nothing about (e.g., a seller who owes more on his house than it will sell for and has no money to cover the difference.) Agents often like to be "social workers"—this results in their spending too much time on issues that they have no power to resolve.

Ask your agents what objections/issues they currently face, and then go to work developing effective answers. Try to develop a few (at least four) different ways to answer each objection, as one answer rarely fits all situations. Go "round robin" so that all agents can participate and feel that they have created the scripts—this will give you have buy-in.

Have someone in these classes record or write down all the different answers, keeping in mind that all scripts need to be in first person. At the end of the class, have your admin staff type up the scripts and give them out to the agents to learn. You can also reuse the scripts you've just developed for future classes.

Don't overlook other key topics for reality-dialogue classes, such as Lead Mastery and SOI. Lead-mastery scripts should address phone, Internet leads, OH, etc. SOI scripts should focus on building relationships and providing value.

## Working Expired Listings

This is another great opportunity for agents to build business. No need to buy anything—just use the script provided, the absorption-rate pricing analysis, and the listing presentation. If you do that—and find a qualified, motivated seller—instead of taking a listing, you'll actually sell one.

### EXPIRED-LISTING DIALOGUE

*Use this same scripting whether going door-to-door or on the phone.*

*"'M/M Seller,'" this is _____ with _____.*
*I saw that your listing with _____ recently expired.*
*I've done the research, and **I know why your home didn't sell.** When would you like to meet to discuss my findings?"*

Use the absorption-rate report to illustrate proper pricing, and then explain market conditions—use stats! And how they have negatively affected the sale of the property—and will continue to do so.

**Important!** When using the above dialogue, *if you have a motivated seller, **take the listing and sell it.*** You have just saved the seller money by selling the property sooner rather than later. **In today's market, time is money.**

# 8

# Miscellaneous Management Objectives

**Management Mindset - The Way We Are Measured Has Changed**
It is important that owners and their management understand the effects of this reality and address this in daily activities.

Are stats a part of your daily dialogue? Do they support your marketing decisions? Do you use them to train, coach and recruit? Put them at the heart of everything. Have your agents internalized them? This is critical.

So how do we address this?

In TRAINING – the backbone of all that we do and stand for. We know that training improves productivity – utilize reality dialogues. There will be no agent implementation – no matter how good your training is – no matter how well agents understand it intellectually if we don't put this into practice – and practice is how we get there from here.

Compute your company stats – DOM, %LS v LT, ASP v OLP and begin .If you are going to gear up your training program effectively – then you must be very clear where you stand competitively in the eyes of the consumer.

Most of this comes back to pricing – in fact they all do – how many of the agents fully comprehend absorption rate analysis pricing AND can communicate it confidently? This component is critical. It illustrates a belief behind the advice and counsel we are proffering – what consumer would buy into anything else in this economic climate?

In COACHING – start focusing more on the stats for the individual agent. The good news is that the numbers offer a real glimpse at reality, no more hedging. One on one is where your real power is with an agent. Know their individual numbers. If the agents' numbers are bad - the overall company numbers will be bad. You cannot afford to let this happen.

Your paradigm shift is back to basics supported by statistics to satisfy a mistrustful consumer. Nothing more.

As you go through and plan all of the elements of your job, infuse statistics at every opportunity. It's a mindset change.

## Sales Meetings

This meeting, which is optimally effective when held weekly or biweekly, is a time for the manager to take control and define the agenda. *This is a **sales** meeting.* I emphasize the seemingly obvious here because I've experienced many so-called sales meetings that actually discouraged selling—literally scaring agents to death about such things as mold and legal issues. Give agents the information they need to know, but stay focused on listing and selling. If necessary, hold a separate meeting to cover information that is not specifically related to sales.

I have provided an outline for effective sales meetings. Text italics provide explanations to help you with implementation.

### SALES-MEETING OUTLINE

*Create a written agenda for each meeting, using a saved template. Take attendance, using a sign-in sheet. Keep meetings upbeat, positive, and fun. **Use the meeting to inspire your agents.** Limit outside speakers remember that this is a **sales** meeting!*

*Be sure to include the list below on every agenda. It's a good idea to save these points (text not in italics) as part of the agenda template.*

- Opening motivation—*begin every meeting with an inspirational quote—preferably a different one for each meeting.*
- Your soapbox—*this should directly follow the quote, and it can include any issue you want to discuss (professionalism, attitude, legal problems, etc.).*
- Recognition—*every month, recognize those who continue to achieve.*
- New business update—*comes next on the agenda, and it should include:*
  o New listings, price reductions, and upcoming listings (*price reductions discussed here are different from the price-reductions meetings held separately—focus on the sales impact here*)
  o New sales (*make sure to address new sales separately*)
- Any current needs—*use your judgment on this; it may or may not vary from meeting to meeting.*
*Always ask agent for the source of business (SOB).*

***The focus is current info—do not allow any agent to talk about old listings!*** *Discussing old listings during a sales meeting gives the agent recognition for not having done the job.*

- Monthly market statistics—*should follow new business and current needs, and should include:*
    Both office and market stats
    SOB percentages

- Mortgages—*this should be a brief in-house LO update (i.e., something that offers an advantage/ benefit to agents and/or consumers).*
- Announcements
- Legal updates
- Training offerings
- Housekeeping issues

*Again, use your judgment on the last four points, which may or may not vary from meeting to meeting.*

- Slide show/virtual tour of new listings—*the practice of tour still exists today, but I question its value, as it allows consumers to find out about new listings before agents do. In today's world this is unacceptable. Inquiries come in, but the agent knows nothing about the property—in essence, they wait for the "Broker Open" to have lunch served in order to preview it.*
- Closing motivation—*always end the sales meeting on an upbeat note. Encourage agents with a positive, sales-oriented statement, such as:*

"Now go out there and sell houses! Remember, you are the best-trained agents in this market."

*Every sales meeting should end within forty-five minutes or less. Make sure you finish the meeting in that time frame. End the meeting when you're done. Respect everyone's time and don't drag out the meeting needlessly.*

## Monthly Market Statistics

This information is critical to business today. Management and agents alike must grasp that in order to have credibility with the consumer they must demonstrate knowledge of market conditions and be able to communicate that information using statistics. No more generalizations or opinions in today's market—just the facts.

The market-statistics analysis requires using the MLS. Management should prepare this report for the first sales meeting of each month, and then have a discussion about how the statistics affect both seller and a buyer, as well as how to advise each them accordingly. (For instance, *"Given what we are seeing in market listing inventory, how should we advise our sellers? What about our buyers?"*)

The discussion should continue until every agent has a clear understanding as to what the statistics actually mean for the buying and selling consumer.

Be sure to include days on market in the analysis. Remember that the DOM stat compares the overall market with the individual office, so you can use it to measure how effective you are at the use of absorption-rate analysis. If your results are superior to your competitors, you have a stat that will set you apart from your competitors. Use it in your presentations, as well as your marketing materials/strategies, in order to demonstrate results that matter to the consumer. (For instance, "The average days on market with our competitors is 141;

this company's DOM is 63—that's a difference of 55 percent! More importantly, we save our sellers nearly three mortgage payments.")

In addition to market statistics, I've included other information vital to any agent/manager conducting business today.

The second section illustrates source of business. You should formulate SOB by using actual data from your office's closed transactions for the month—this way, no agent can say that the information is not relevant to him or her. Now you have the stats for what's working in the marketplace, and any agent whose business is off track can see what to do to change that fact. SOB numbers also provide backup for your marketing proposals – little need for print media when only @ 2 percent of our business originates there.

The third part of the form addresses the generational breakdown of your customers. Again, compiled from your office's actual closed business, these stats tell you who your customers are—as well as how adaptive you need to be to generational expectations that differ from what you may consider to be the norm.

I've added % of **L**istings **S**old for the office – a collective reminder of how well we are doing the job we are hired to do.

% of Distressed Sales measures shorts sales and foreclosures closed in your market – NAR got this right – "all markets are different".

Taken collectively, after a thorough explanation and discussion of the information on this form, you can now explain market conditions to both agents and consumers by *using statistics.* These stats will let you know where your business is coming from currently, who your customer is, and how adaptive you need to be to generational differences. All this information is critical to anyone doing business in real estate today.

Provide this information consistently, and teach agents (and Management) how to use them to support advice they provide consumers  and management will increase in value to the company's agents.

*Note that some available software programs can provide very detailed information concerning market conditions, but most of these programs use graphs and other visual representations. My advice is this: Keep it simple. Most agents are not "numbers people," and because they don't necessarily understand the information when presented in this format, they are also unable to explain it. If they can't explain it, they won't explain it. If they use the information at all, they will just give it to the seller or buyer, who will have to wade through it/decipher it without professional guidance or commentary. To reiterate,* **agents must grasp market conditions and their implications for consumers, and then be able to communicate all of this effectively.**

*[Form follows.]*

# MONTHLY MARKET STATS

**Month**                                                  **Office**

_____                    _____

| In **your market** area: | 2011 | _vs._ | 2010 | % Difference |
|---|---|---|---|---|
| # Listing Inventory | _____ | | _____ | _____ |
| # Under Contract | _____ | | _____ | _____ |
| # Closed Sales | _____ | | _____ | _____ |
| Avg. Sales Price | _____ | | _____ | _____ |

DOM  _____ (mkt.)  _____ (co.)  _____

Distressed Sales  _____% (mkt)    Listings Sold  _____% (co) _____% (mkt)

## By Office

## SOB

| | |
|---|---|
| SOI | _____% |
| Marketing effort | _____% |
| Internet | _____% |
| Company | _____% |

## Generational Breakdown

| | |
|---|---|
| 66 and over | _____% |
| 47–65 | _____% |
| 31–46 | _____% |
| 14–30 | _____% |

## Leads-Management System

**First,** determine which leads you will—and will not—charge a referral fee. Be clear.

**Second**, establish agent eligibility requirements (see below) for leads.

**Third**, establish a system for lead incubation for company use after the agent has tried three times with no success converting the lead. The agent must be able to **respond immediately,** or you will **immediately reassign** the lead to another agent who is available.

Develop a thorough job description for the staff person handling leads management. Compensate this position with a base salary, plus a bonus (i.e., $25/deal closed).

Announce the new leads-management system at least thirty days in advance of its rollout in order to give all agents an opportunity to qualify for eligibility.

Develop a database for leads. Separate leads from the web from other leads. Go back twelve months to retrieve leads for management system.

Script responses for follow-up. Train agents on "Lead Mastery" questions/responses. Here are some response examples:
**First response:** "Based on where you are in your property search, what information can I provide that will be most helpful to you at this point?"

**Biweekly e-mail responses:** First, send "Monthly Market Stats" section for year-over-year market activity. Second e-mail can include the percentage of distressed sales for your market. Use the same responses each month, until the consumer directs/requests otherwise. Include in the e-mail responses: "If you need more specific statistics for a different market area, let us know. We're happy to help."

Track the percentage of leads converted—overall and by individual agent—in order to measure effectiveness. Also track the percentage of your leads marked "dead."

**Remember, no system can work without follow-up by staff to confirm that the responding agent met the consumers' needs.**

**Agent Eligibility Requirements**

Determine the production requirement for getting leads. Always reward your productive agents—you'll get better conversion.

The time frame for production requirements can range anywhere within the previous thirty to sixty days. You can define a *transaction* as a listing taken, a listing sold, a ratified buyer side sale, or a closed sale.

Your current production will guide your parameters. For example, if you have few producing agents, then you'll have to extend the time frame in order to include more people and adequately cover your leads. You can also define *production* as anything that has had any one of the types of production listed.

If you have a large office with strong production, you should make your requirements tougher. For example, production in the previous thirty days, and decide on a listing sold or a buyer side ratified contract.

Make training a requirement. Using "Leads Mastery" as reality practice training. The agent must demonstrate agility in using the appropriate questions in response to consumer needs.

*It isn't about the number of visitors; it's about percentage of conversion.* **Focus on the consumer**—*it's about them (consumers), not us (brokers/agents).*

## Policies-and-Procedures (P&P) Manual

Having an up-to-date policies–and-procedures (P&P) manual is a necessity. The P&P manual provides is a guide that explains the day-to-day operations of your company/office, as well as detailing management directives, etc. It can answer many "got a minute" questions. Finally,  it can—and should—make sure you appear fair and equitable (i.e., that you do not play "favorites").

**Suggested P&P Topics**
Administrative staff job descriptions
Advertising—supply a copy of any form needed for submission
Agency (buyer, seller, sub and/or dual)
Agent commission on personal real-estate transactions
Assistants

Awards
Blogs
Commission schedule
Copiers
Customer service
Disclosure forms
Do-not-call list
Dress code
E-mail
E&O
Ethics and legal
Fax
Floor duty
Home services/preferred vendors
Insurance—minimum requirement
Leads management
Licensure
Lockboxes
Mailings
Minimum production standard
Mortgage
Multiple offers
Non-compete clause
Postage
Property tours/caravan
Referrals—inbound and outbound; among your own agents
Sales meetings
Sexual harassment
Signs, riders
Smoking
Social media
Team policy
Technology
Termination
Title
Training—requirements for new and experienced
Transaction coordination/listings and sales
Transaction coordinators
Vacations
Website

Be clear and concise in your language and direction! Also, be thorough. Consider one issue at a time. Before you write the policy/procedure, think about what you want each one to look like and how you want the entire system/operation to work. Make sure you align your P&P with your state and local laws (and federal laws, if applicable).

**Make sure <u>every agent reads</u> the P&P manual, and then <u>signs</u> a form stating that he or she read and understood all the policies and procedures outlined.** *Keep every agent's signed form in his or her personnel file.*

Date the P&P with revisions, as necessary; every agent must sign a new form as revisions occur (file these new signoffs in the personnel files).

## Price-Reductions Meetings

*Use this directive monthly, either in place of one of your coaching meetings or as a way to ease into establishing a coaching program. Information discussed during these meetings should differ from, and be more detailed than, that which you discuss during sales meetings relative to this topic.*

Print out your office listing inventory by individual agent.

Have agents redo the "Absorption-Rate Analysis Report" for each of their listings and bring the revised version to the meeting.

Meet with each agent (again, can take the place of coaching session) and go over each listing on the market for more than thirty days.

For each listing, ask, *"Where do we need to price this listing in order to sell it in the next thirty days?"*

Give a specific directive on price reductions for each listing.

**Review price-reduction format:**

- Re-qualify seller (*as to motivation*).
- Ask for the price reduction—*use absorption rate; handle objections; make sure it's not a condition.*
- Obtain the price reduction.
<u>or</u>

- Terminate the listing—*make the necessary business decision, but do so nicely in order to leave the door open for the future (sample script follows).*

> *"'Mr./Ms Seller,' I am returning your listing to you because I cannot do the job you have hired me to do. Given the current market absorption-rate analysis, the price position of your home will not attract today's buyer. If you change your mind about pricing your home to sell, I'll be happy to work with you again."*

Even if you only reduce half your listings, you will be ahead of the game—and it will show up on your bottom line and that of the agents.

As our competitive advantage is increasingly measured by the statistics that support that we can get the job done today – the ability to get a listing sold becomes more important.

## Agent Business Book Club and Reading List

Mark Twain said it best: "The man who does not read has no advantage over the man who cannot read."

Conduct the Agent Business Book Club on a monthly basis. It can be an effective change agent. At every meeting, the book's author becomes the trainer in the room. I have seen the book club change entire office cultures by improving their understanding of business issues. As we work to develop our agents as businesspeople, the book club can be a valuable tool. Depending on the topic, it is also a way to demonstrate interest in the agent on a personal development level as well.

Assign one book per month, making it clear that every agent is responsible for buying the book.

Hold a roundtable discussion during which you apply the lessons learned to their business and/or personal growth.

Let the agents drive the discussion. Management should only jump in when it is necessary to get the discussion back on track.

Book selection will reflect current issues and time-of-year application.

Announce upcoming meeting two weeks in advance, by e-mail and at the sales meeting.

*[Suggested reading list follows, in alphabetical order by title.]*

## Reading List

| | |
|---|---|
| *Blink* | Gladwell |
| *Content Matters* | Handley and Chapman |
| *Daily Six* | Chappelear |
| *Drive* | Pink |
| *E Myth Revisited* | Gerber |
| *Execution* | Bossidy/Charan |
| Facebook Era | Clara Shih |
| *Failing Forward* | Maxwell |
| *First Things First* | Covey |
| *FISH* | Lundin |
| *Go Givers Sell More* | Burg, Mann |
| *Good to Great* | Collins |
| *How to Win Friends and Influence People* | Carnegie |
| *Know-How* | Char an |
| *Let's Get Real or Let's Not Play* | Khalsa and Illig |
| *Made to Stick* | Heath |
| *Outliers* | Gladwell |
| *Purpose-Driven Life* | Warren |
| *Raving Fans* | Blanchard |
| Rework | Fried and Hansson |
| *Sales Dogs* | Singer |
| *Satisfaction* | Powers, DeNove |
| *Seven Habits of Highly Effective People* | Covey |
| *Smart Couples Finish Rich* | Bach |
| *Smart Women Finish Rich* | Bach |
| Switch | Heath(s) |
| *Talent Is Overrated* | Colvin |
| The Digital Handshake | Paul Chaney |
| *The Dip* | Godin |
| *The Gold Book of YES/Attitude* | Gitomer |
| *The Hundred Year Lie* | Fitzgerald |
| *The Levity Effect* | Gostick |

| | |
|---|---|
| The Little Big Things | Tom Peters |
| *The Little Black Book of Connections* | Gitomer |
| *The Little Red Book of Sales Answers* | Gitomer |
| *The Little Red Book of Selling* | Gitomer |
| *The Long Tail* | Anderson |
| *The New Rules of Marketing and PR* | Scott |
| The New World of Wireless | Scott Snyder |
| *The Platinum Rule for Sales Mastery* | Alessandra, Zimmerman, LaLopa |
| *The Platinum Rule* | Alessandra |
| *The Secret* | Byrne |
| *The Upside* | Slywotsky |
| *The Winning Spirit* | Montana |
| *The World Is Flat* (revised edition) | Friedman |
| *Think and Grow Rich* | Hill |
| *Tipping Point* | Gladwell |
| *Tribes* | Seth Godin |
| *Trust Agents* | Brogan and Smith |
| *Turn Clicks Into Clients* | Forrester |
| *What Clients Love* | Beckwith |
| *What Got You Here Won't Get You There* | Marshall Goldsmith |
| *What to Say When You Talk to Yourself* | Helmstetter |
| *Who Moved My Cheese?* | Johnson/Blanchard |
| *Wired to Care* | Paitnaik |
| *Working with Emotional Intelligence* | Goleman |

*To be continued . . .*

# Exit Interviews

Conduct an exit interview whenever you lose a manager, an agent, or an administrative employee. State in your P&P Manual that this interview is mandatory, specifying that the employee will not receive final compensation until after the exit interview. In addition, for agents, specify that you will not return the agent's license to the state until after the exit interview.

You can gain valuable information from exit interviews, and you can use that information to help prevent future losses. You can't fix what you don't know is broken.

## EXIT INTERVIEW

When did you start looking for another job/office, and why?

As you look back over your experiences here, did they match your expectations when you first joined the company? Explain.

What would be the one change that I could have made to significantly improve your experience here?

What would you say was your most significant contribution to this company?

What was your most significant disappointment?

Is there anything else that you would like me to know?

## Agent Advisory Committee

*The Agent Advisory Committee addresses retention and morale issues. This committee enables agents to feel that they have input in the decision-making process. It also keeps management informed about what's going on, and as a result, it can be instrumental in preventing issues from becoming overblown.*

Take a count of your existing agents, and then figure out how many committee members you'll want. (Approximately 10 percent is usually effective; e.g., 35 agents = 3–5 members.) Elect an odd number for voting purposes.

Group agents by production levels and have all agents vote for one agent in each category. Also, consider the generational makeup of the committee.

Every committee member should have a maximum one-year term.

Hold committee meetings monthly at a specific time (e.g., the second Thursday of every month at 1 p.m. Publish a schedule of meetings for the entire year.

Make sure to remind your agents of upcoming meetings, letting them know that if they have a topic for discussion, they should submit it to a committee member.

Have committee members to report on any findings, decisions, etc., that result from agents' submissions at your next sales meetings.

**Impress upon committee members that some discussions are confidential— and that breach of any confidential matter will result in termination from the committee.**

<u>Caution!</u> Make sure that you address all issues and respond to them accordingly—even when you will not take any action, and/or when action is not necessary. Agents want to know that you listen to and consider their opinions and concerns.

## Customer Satisfaction

More than ever before, customer satisfaction is at the heart of what we need to deliver if we want to be effective. As an industry, we do little in this area. Most of the time, we lag behind, fighting the changes that occur in consumer preferences. The industry has to understand that the consumer pays our bills—and in order to thrive, we have to understand what they think and want, and why.

Franchises, as well as some companies, do have customer surveys that they e-mail to buyers and sellers following transactions. However, the response rate to these is frequently low; as a result, we are unaware of what a large percentage of our customers think.

In order to protect company reputations in the marketplace, responding to consumer wants and needs is critical. Turn them into advocates for the services we provide. This is difficult, because no two agents can give the same response to what customer satisfaction actually means.

> One of my past clients had received top franchise customer-service awards for more than fourteen consecutive years—only to have one agent destroy that record. The reason? That agent's response to <u>customer dissatisfaction</u> was this: "I didn't do anything wrong." That agent was also a top producer.

Wouldn't it be great if we compensated agents based on their ability to do their jobs well, **from the consumer's perspective**?

### Customer-Satisfaction Follow-up

### Get on the phone!

Prior to making customer-satisfaction follow-up phone calls, check the consumer's file. It should contain a completed form with all pertinent information relative to the transaction; either you, or the staffer you delegate the task to, should complete this form after final processing of the transaction, and then put it in the consumer's file. **Whoever makes the follow-up call must review this form first.** If you delegate making the calls, ensure that the staffer knows to give you an immediate heads-up if any problem arises, so that you can take appropriate action.

Again, either management or staff can make the phone calls—depending on the number of closings you enjoy—**but you must make these calls!** Set aside an hour or two each week, and call the previous week's buyers and sellers to find out how they feel about the job you and your agents did. Script it something like this:

*"Hello, 'Mr./Ms. Buyer/Seller.' This is _____ with _____. Congratulations on your sale/purchase. (Use the actual address of the property bought/sold.)*

*"I'm calling to find out how you feel about the job we did for you during the transaction.* **(Listen** *to the response before continuing.)*

*"Is there anything we could have done differently or in addition to the level of service we provided? Was there any part of the transaction that proved especially stressful for you?* **(Listen** *carefully and learn from the responses.)*

**If you are willing to listen and learn, you can become extraordinary at what you do.** But you can't learn if you become defensive while listening to the response—or afterward. While speaking with the consumer, probe for more info so that you completely understand what happened and the consumer's reactions to that. Fix what's broken!

*Whether you speak to the consumer directly, or receive a heads-up from the staffer you have delegated the task to,* ***the key to effective customer-satisfaction is that you must*** <u>***respond immediately***</u>*.* You won't be able to fix all situations, but apologies are powerful—and people do remember them!

## Sale of Agent's Book of Business

Sale of an agent's book of business helps the productive agent to transition out of real estate. **An agent who has not stayed in touch with his or her SOI regularly may not have anything to sell** (which is why only productive agents' transitions warrant such sales).

Establish a time frame for the transition—it's best to start a year in advance of the transition.

Determine the qualities/strengths of the agent candidate seeking to purchase the book of business. It can become problematic if the retiring agent decides to "sell" to an agent with a different working style (i.e., dissimilar initiative, work ethic, etc.), as the agent who steps into the client base will not work it in a similar fashion to the retiring agent. Consider generational differences, too.

Develop a written job description with online checklists, as needed. Job moves forward with time/experience/results.

Develop a compensation model (i.e., 40 percent; 30 percent; 20 percent, referral over three years). Put the agreed terms in writing, signed by both agents.

Disseminate and/or post a partnership announcement (i.e., send a letter or e-mail; post on website and/or social media) twelve months prior to effective date.

Market SOI monthly, incorporating all marketing pieces (i.e., photos, website, cards, signs, ads, etc.).

Involve the buying agent in the workings of his or her business, including listing presentations, negotiations, follow-up calls, etc.

Send/post official announcement of agent's retirement. Do this sixty days in advance, and again thirty days later.

Make final phone calls to entire SOI. Retiring agent needs to personally call each person to express thanks for all the trust, and referrals, over the years. He or she should end the call with something like: "I hope that you will continue to let _____ (*use the name of agent buying the book of business*) help you in the future."

You need to make it clear to the retiring agent that you expect him or her to continue to work the SOI monthly in order to provide consistency during the transition and afterwards.

## The Issue of Teams

Brokers face a number of issues because of the emergence of teams in real estate. The biggest one is that many teams are not profitable for the broker; they only benefit the team leader. In addition, the broker may have little knowledge of team practices, dynamics, etc.,—yet the broker has a legal responsibility for the team's actions.

Today's management would do well to ask why real-estate companies/offices establish teams in the first place. Various companies and trainers support the establishment of teams—it's a living—and some brokers believe that it reduces their recruiting responsibilities, which may or may not prove to be true. **Regardless, if establishing teams doesn't add to the bottom line, why do it?**

*If you allow teams, you **must establish clear policies** for them.* How do you handle training team members? Who is responsible for their training? Do team members receive coaching? If so, from whom? What is the split/commission schedule for team members? Who gets the production credit? Are team leaders allowed to recruit to their team from your agent population? What is the expectation for using ancillary services?

Most teams exist because of insufficient, or non-existent, leadership strength at the top. Management do not train or coach the agents to produce, so they join teams, hoping that something will trickle down to them—even at much-reduced splits. Many agents believe that team leaders have more on the ball than their managing brokers. **Provide skilled management, and you will reduce—if not eliminate—the need and desire for teams!**

In effect, team leaders (I am not referring to agent partnerships) put together companies within companies. They have the level of administrative help they want and need, and so they hire lesser-producing agents to handle the business they don't want to handle (usually buyers).

While plenty of large teams—some the size of companies— do exist, I recommend that brokers counsel any agent thinking of forming a team to first hire an assistant (transaction coordinators can substitute), as agents asking to establish a team usually seek admin support. When production warrants, he or she can ask another interested agent in the office to take buyer referrals. Set the referral fee upfront and in writing. Determine expected business practices, etc. By doing this, instead of establishing actual teams, the would-be "team leader" avoids losing the buyer's agent when he or she is strong enough to work independently, which in turn prevents having to rehire, retrain, etc. The agent can concentrate on production instead.

# 9

# Time Management

How do you make your plan a reality? Manage your activities Monday through Friday. Many broker owners lack the ability to efficiently manage their time. Many are working long and hard. The question that I pose to you is this: "How much of your time do you spend on the things that result in a profit and create growth?"

Time management can make the difference—it is what will allow you accomplish your goals and objectives, and also what will help you avoid burnout and bankruptcy.

Learn to treat every activity that is necessary in order for you to reach your goals and objectives as if it were an appointment. Schedule everything. Whether it is a personal or professional activity, assign it a time frame. Treat everything as you would if you had an actual scheduled appointment.

## Creating a Schedule

Learn to carve out a productive routine for yourself. In order to accomplish that, you must consider the following:

- On average, at what time do you arrive at the office every day?
- How much time does it take you to set up and organize yourself for the day?
- Prepare your schedule on a two-week basis. *(As a general rule, you can usually cover all your activities in a two-week period.)*
- Plan your meeting/training/coaching schedule:

    o   First, consider your total number of agents.

    o   Next, consider the number of agents you need to coach on a regular basis. Allow for twenty-minute meetings—weekly, biweekly, and monthly.

    o   Finally, work each item in blocks of time; you'll manage your time better and find that it's easy to establish and maintain a routine.

- Block out the time you'll need each day *(i.e., coaching six agents a day requires two hours of your time)*.

- How many of your agents prospect daily? In the morning or afternoon? Don't schedule your meetings to conflict with their schedule.

- Are you a "morning" or "afternoon" person? Schedule coaching and recruiting in the time frame during which you feel most energetic, alert, and comfortable— do the things that are most important when you are at your best!

- Allow time to make the necessary number of contacts for recruiting every day.
  - Factor in the number of weeks you'll work, which is equal to the time available to do the work.
  - Determine the necessary number of contacts you must make every day. *(To do this, multiply the number of agents you need to hire by eighty; divide that number by the number of weeks you'll work; and finally, divide that number by the number of days per week that you'll make calls. For every twenty contacts, you should get one appointment. For every four appointments, you should average one hire.)*

- Other activities/needs to consider for optimal time management (per each two-week period):
  o Number of hours you spend in training programs
  o Number of hours you spend coaching
  o Number of hours you spend in sales meetings
  o Number of hours spend in tour/caravan
  o Number of hours you spend in management meetings
  o Number of hours you spend on board activities
  o Number of hours you spend on special projects
  o Number of hours you need to take care of personal business

Add anything else you need to schedule during a two-week period—if you encounter a one-time special circumstance for any given period, you still should add it. *Simply put, you need to* **schedule all your activities as appointments,** *and then make sure that you treat them as such.*

Now that you have made a list (if you need to extend the list past two weeks in order to include everything critical that you know is coming up, you can do so), start plugging your activities into your schedule. Remember to work in blocks of time and complete the most important things early in the day before the "got a minute?" requests start.

**Sample Schedule**

| | |
|---|---|
| 8:30 a.m. | Arrive at office; return calls and e-mails. |
| 9–10 a.m. | Make recruiting calls. |
| 10–11a.m. | Sales Meeting or Agent Training class |
| 11 a.m.–12 p.m. | Coach three agents (*twenty minutes each*) |
| 12–1 p.m. | Lunch |
| 1–2 p.m. | Coach three agents (*twenty minutes each*) |
| 2–5:30 p.m. | Open (*you can use this time for whatever you need to do, i.e., schedule recruiting appointments; prepare sales meeting agenda; review files; return calls and e-mails, etc.*) |

Obviously, not all days are created equal. You may have to add "Management Meeting," etc.—not to mention the need to be flexible for emergencies—the point is to schedule as much as you possibly can. When you do, you will find it easier to handle any emergencies that you have not/could not schedule in advance.

*If you followed this sample schedule for one week, you would have accomplished the following: conducted thirty coaching meetings; spent five hours making recruiting contacts; held one sales meeting; conducted four training classes.* **How much closer to reaching your goals and activities would you be as a result of completing these activities?**

# 10

# Technology

Technology is an essential tool in today's marketplace. Both young and not-so-young consumers use technology for the information they want and need—before they begin to even think about contacting a real-estate agent. This is an arena that will continue to grow and change as the younger consumer becomes a more viable component of the housing market.

## Websites

In response to the increased use of technology as a necessary tool, companies and agents alike have sunk significant dollars in developing websites and Internet strategies in the hopes of attracting the consumer.

According to Google Alerts (as of the end of 2010), this is how our industry websites fared:

> Visits Per Day: Industry average = 100
>
> Total Page Views: Industry average = 600
>
> Average Pages/Visit: Industry average = 4
>
> Average Time on Site: Industry average = ~3 minutes
>
> Average Bounce Rate: Industry average = ~45 percent

No matter what your technological know-how might be, you can see that these results are abysmal. The only numbers worse than these are our lead-conversion rates, which for most are nonexistent.

Your website is your face to the world, at first glance. It is a necessary and useful tool, because, in addition to creating your "first impression," it serves the consumers' needs and wants. Your SOI check you out online before contacting agents — they want to ensure that you have a substantial web presence.

*I ask clients to think of a place where they think they might like to retire. I tell them to search for the information they might need in order to make a move by finding the website that gives it to them—easily and without obligation, because that is what the best informational websites do.*

In short, **give consumers what they want, and they will follow.** Make sure your website does what the developer who designed it set it up to do (which should be in line with your instructions/requirements). Have policies that ensure that each of your listings appears with full information, complete with virtual tours and/or photo slideshows. Have at least eight links that the consumer can use for additional information. Have you included market stats – updated monthly - on your website? The consumer is looking. Are they a part of your email signature? The consumer is checking. If not, you will loose the opportunity to compete – an opportunity you never knew you had – they won't bother to contact you if they don't find the stats when they check.

**Common RE website flaws:**
- **No photos/tours**—why post a listing without photos/tours? (*Consumers won't even glance at a site without photos, and think of how you are **not** serving your seller clients!*)
- **Lack of complete information**—no depth on mortgage, community, neighborhood, recreation, health care, schools, shopping, churches, transportation, services/activities for seniors, etc.
- Unanswered inquires
- No maps or area tours
- Unable to view all listing inventory until they sort through your listings.
- No market stats
- Not interactive enough
- Few links
- No vendor links
- No OH (open house) information
- No useful blogs

Recommended reading for websites: *Real Estate Rainmaker: Guide to Online Marketing* by Dan Gooder Richard. This book is still timely and can save you money.

I ask clients to use the enhanced version of *Realtor.com*— it's where the majority of 40 year + consumers go first. **The point is to be where the consumer is.**

*Zillow.com* and *Trulia.com* are close runners-up, and younger consumers seem to prefer these two sites. Remember generational differences! Track the consumer numbers to know when changes in consumer preferences occur, so that you can follow them.

Find someone who can build you a website that does what it is supposed to do, and then make sure to update the site on a regular basis. Check weekly to see where your company appears on search pages. If you're not on the first page, you lose.

That said, will the best website ever take the place of the skill and services a trained professional brings to the transaction? Do we think that that may have something to do with our low lead-capture rate? You bet!

Train your agents to understand Internet consumers and to respond to them effectively, and your capture rate will increase. Use "Leads Mastery" and "Monthly Market Stats" information in your reality-dialogue classes; otherwise, you'll lose the advantage that a solid website and well-trained agents can give you.

Review your leads-management system and revise policies, as needed, in order to increase lead conversion.

## Social Media

Don't underestimate the power of social media – this is huge! Called the "social economy" and "socioeconomics" – this is not going away. In fact, it's grown much bigger much faster than most envisioned. The trend now is that major companies and industry will be joining our postings – we will see a more professional approach to videos and postings. The fine line is being able to communicate without directly marketing to the consumer.

New ways to communicate evolve continually, and consumers excel at using them—far more so than we do. At best, we play catch-up. Social media/networking sites abound—Facebook, YouTube, LinkedIn, Twitter, Blogs.com, etc.—and they are free! These sites and many more allow us to increase communication with the consumer and provide new opportunities for growth.

Most of us are beyond print advertising—the fact that newspaper readership is shrinking has awakened us from the long sleep that allowed us to rely solely (or at least primarily) on print ads to market our listings.

Again, you'll find and attract consumers by using social media – Facebook has over 500 million users. These platforms allow consumers to choose what they want to read and who they want to communicate with—and give guidance and referrals on services and purchases.

Follow these guidelines when posting:

- Consider the audience you want
- Post to develop followers – it takes time
- Use pictures and videos to enhance your postings
- Use a real estate related post weekly
- Include lots of community related postings
- Make your page distinctive
- Facebook – casual photo – consumer to consumer
- LinkedIn – business photo – business to business

Be careful not to view these platforms as vehicles for advertising or marketing—that's not what they are, and you will lose your opportunity to communicate with an unlimited number of people if you go that route. It is genuine give-and-take. It's about sharing. It will benefit you to remember that social media is only one part of a consumer-centric response.

Plan a strategy: think first about who you want your audience to be. Engage them. Give them something of interest that will spark a repost or a conversation and make them want to return.

**Examples of successful weekly posts:**

**Week one:** post your market stats for the previous month – use percentages for clarity.
**Week two**: post about an activity (training etc.) that you have offered/attended. Use video.
**Week three**: post % of distressed sales for the previous month in your market.
**Week four**: again, focus on activities, articles or community info. Use videos. Ask questions.

Posting on social media sites should take no more than 60 minutes a week. Just use the suggested postings over and over. The consumer wants numbers – so give them.

Suggested wording:
"For those of you out there that follow the market stats for Fairfax County, December looked like this: Your thoughts?"

Pay attention to what gets comments or "likes" and let that be your guide – even the experts are in uncharted waters here – focus on learning from your successes.

**Monitor your social media accounts:**

www.Nutshellmail.com **and** www.constantcontact.com/socialmedia

## Marketing around Property Listings
*In other words, how can we drive more traffic to our websites?*

- *Postlets.com*—syndicate listings *with your contact info.*
    o   Post to Craigslist, Facebook, and numerous other sites.

- *Trulia.com*—claim listings (yours and unclaimed ones).
    o   Claim the listings attached to your e-mail address.
    o   Search for properties by ZIP code or city.
    o   Find which listings have no contact info (unclaimed).
    o   Manually load unclaimed listings to your account.
    o   Participate in "Trulia Voices," which answer consumer questions.
    o   Set up "alerts" to decide which questions and ZIP code(s) you want to cover.

- *Zillow.com*—claim listings that use the exact same e-mail address attached to the syndicated listing.
    o   Create a complete profile that links back to your website and/or blog.

- *ListingBook.com*—customer-relationship management (CRM) tool.
    o   Sign up clients, prospects, neighbors, etc.—literally anyone who wants to search  "like an agent."
    o   Monitor the criteria and frequency of use, make comments on the properties, etc.

- ***Twitter.com***—this is a micro blogging site that can be used to promote individual listings, blog posts, and other resources. The key to effective use of Twitter ("tweeting") is daily use and monitoring.

I have touched on some of the main sites and key issues with technology, but I am not an expert. I do understand enough about it to know that even the best technology will not make up for poor lead-conversion skills or the industry know-how we must have in order to effectively do our jobs.

Learn what to use and how to use it. Consult the best experts available. (I highly recommend Catherine Read: www.creativeread.com). She knows her stuff and can communicate it to brokers and agents alike.)

# 11

# Administrative Staff

Good admin staff is the foundation of a well-run office. If you lack good admin support—for both you and your agents—you will not be able to grow your office to full potential. You will involve yourself in the admin work, and your own work will suffer. You will have no time to recruit, coach, and train.

## Job Descriptions

Put together job descriptions for each position. Ask each staff member to write out his or her current job description—this will help you to finalize each description and correct any discrepancies that exist.

Have each staff member put together a notebook that details what he or she does, and when he or she does it. This is sort of a daily operations guide, as opposed to a job description, and it can serve as a "training manual" for each position. Make sure these notebooks receive necessary updates, as needed—you never know when you might unexpectedly need to fill a position.

## Current Staff Assessment

Begin by assessing your current administrative staff individually. Most employees fall into one of three types. Consider the following:

1. Semi-qualified, dependent on direction, unreliable

2. Qualified, reasonably independent, reliable

3. Qualified, shows initiative, works independently, reliable.

Best of scenarios is that you have an office staff of "threes". Terminate the "ones", train the "twos" and cherish the "threes" Place the right people in the right jobs. Hold staff accountable making certain that staff knows what you expect and when you expect it.

Having and keeping good admin staff is difficult—RE pay scales aren't the best, and many companies/offices do not offer benefits. If you have good staff, keep them! It will cost you more in the long run to keep rehiring and retraining, and in the end, you won't have the competence that you once did. When I had great admin staff that I couldn't afford to pay well, I would offer other perks, such as extra time off, just as long as they had completed all necessary work.

When hiring new staff, use the interview. Adapt it to the position you want to fill.

*[Form follows.]*

# ADMINISTRATIVE INTERVIEW

Name:                                          Date:

Tell me about yourself.



Describe your knowledge and/or work experience.



What responsibilities did you have?



What did you like most about the jobs you've held?



What computer/bookkeeping/phone skills do you have? What systems/software have you used? In what areas do you have special expertise?



If you could create the perfect job for yourself, what would it be? Where do you see yourself in the next two to three years?



Who was your favorite boss? Why?

Who was your least-favorite boss? Why?

What do you think both bosses would say about you?

Can you think of a time when you went "above and beyond" at work?

If you could change one thing about yourself, what would it be?

How would you handle a difficult/angry consumer/agent?

Tell me about a time when your workload was extremely hectic. How did you handle the situation? What was the outcome?

What have you done in the past to contribute to a supportive environment?

What makes you think you'd be good at the job I've outlined?

What is the most effective way for you to learn new job responsibilities?

What concerns/questions do you have at this point?

Could you give me three references (other than family)?

When could you start work? Is transportation an issue?

What's the best way to contact you?

**<u>Always</u> check references!** Ask the following question: "Would you hire this person again?" Given the fear of employment-law issues, this is the only question you can safely ask that will tell you whether, or not, this may be a good hire.

## Coordinator Staff Positions

In addition to basic staff positions, many companies have been able to offer a higher level of support to their agents in the form of various transaction coordinators. These staff positions allow the agent to concentrate on listing and selling, without the administrative aspects of those transactions bogging them down. Another benefit that is often overlooked——but, which, in my opinion, is the most important—is that these staff positions ensure consistent follow-up with all clients. Be aware that this follow-up is *company follow-up,* even though whichever staff member completes it does so on behalf of the agent.

Most important of all, this follow-up increases the contact between company and consumer.

Depending on your transaction volume, you may choose to combine parts of the Transaction Coordinator and the Listing Coordinator job descriptions. One coordinator should be able to handle forty transactions per month.

### Transaction Coordinator (TC)

Establish this position when agent production increase warrants this additional support. It is customary for agents to pay a fee for each transaction closed. This position also ensures that each of the company's clients receives consistent follow-up and service. I recommend that the TC hold a real-estate license. Have business cards printed so that the agent can give them as he or she introduces the consumer to TC, explaining the coordinator's role in the transaction. Make sure the TC calls to make a by-phone introduction upon receiving the consumer's file.  This introduction increases the comfort level between the TC and the client.

The TC handles the transaction from contract ratification through closing; coordinates home inspection, pest inspection, the loan process, and settlement and title work; and schedules the walk-through and the closing. In addition, the TC keeps the client, agent, and co-broke agent up-to-date on and informed of all events. Post updates by email. Finally, the TC handles customer-service follow-up calls.

The TC receives a base salary and a bonus for each closed transaction:  Base salary of $30,000.00; plus 480 transactions closed annually at $25.00/each – equals $12,000.00 in closed-transaction bonus pay; results in total annual income of $42,000.00. You will need to add the cost of any company benefits in order to determine the total amount of annual compensation. Adjust this pricing for your market conditions.

### Marketing/Listing Coordinator (MC/LC)

*Establish this position as production warrants. Benefits are consistent service, marketing pieces of a higher caliber, and increased time for the agent to list and sell. Agents pay the fee at the time they take the listing.*

The MC handles listings from the time taken until ratified contract, taking care of all details, such as: entering property into MLS and appropriate websites; handling photos/virtual tour and signage; installing lockbox; coordinating agent feedback (recommend using e-mail). MC also handles all marketing and updates clients on a weekly basis; notifies agent at four weeks for price reduction and ten days prior to listing expiration; handles customer-service follow-up calls. Depending on transaction volume, MC can also prepare listing packages and JLJS lists for calls and/or mailings, as well as coordinating tours (if appropriate).

MC receives a base salary and a bonus for each listing taken and each listing closed: Base salary of $35,000.00; plus, 500 listings taken annually at $15.00/each equals $7,500.00 bonus for listings taken for a total compensation of $37,500.00.You will need to add the cost of any benefits in order to determine the amount of total annual compensation. Adjust pricing to your market.

Another way to compensate these staff positions is to pay a flat amount for each closed transaction (i.e., $150.00 for each transaction), with no base salary.

When you put together staff compensation packages, figure best- and worst-case scenarios for all the positions receiving bonus pay. Based on a high and a low number of transactions, figure the total dollar amount. If it's fair, you won't have to revisit the issue.

## Staff Meetings

Hold regular staff meetings—determine the frequency by the competency of your staff and the organization of your office, and hold these a minimum of twice a month.

Put together a file folder on each member of your staff, and place in the file anything you want to go over with that person. Also make a note of anything you have asked that person to do, along with a date for completion. All too often, we expect staff to read our minds and complete tasks in our time frame—but we're the only ones who know what that time frame is. If you have/find a staff member who is able to anticipate you, that is wonderful. I think most of those people went the way of the service staff to the British aristocracy. In today's business world, tell your staff what you expect and when you expect completion.

Having a fully staffed office with competent support staff also leads to agent retention. If your agents fully engage with staff services, little need arises for agent assistants—as these relationships can create too much independence. If an agent has to re-create dependable staff services in order to make a move out of your office, it's less likely that he or she will make the move.

## Staff Reviews

Do regular staff reviews at least semiannually. Staff needs attention, and they want to know that you listen to their ideas and opinions. The review can also ensure that you consider their pay increases in a timely way and do not overlook these increases.

*[Form follows.]*

# ADMINISTRATIVE REVIEW

Name:                                         Date:

How do you feel about what you've accomplished this year?

What are you learning/changing to adapt to current market conditions?

What are your priorities/goals? What challenges do you have?

What skills do you need to upgrade in order to accomplish your objectives?

How can I help?

# 12

# Affiliated/Core Services

Most companies have developed affiliated services—mortgage, title/escrow, insurance, etc. — which they refer to as "core services." I can't quite bring myself to call them core services because capture rate illustrates that they are anything but that.

These affiliated services can create additional and necessary profit centers. The downside of these services—aside from the fact that most don't work very well—is that having additional profit centers has allowed most companies to ignore the biggest hurdle we face: namely, improving the basic real-estate services and skills we offer the buying and selling consumer through our agent community.

## Mortgage

First, see an attorney well versed in RESPA (Real Estate Settlement Procedures Act)—and make sure you understand the act's provisions and restrictions.

**Choose the Right Partner**—I recommend that you partner with a lender that your agents already use; doing so makes the "sale" easier, because the confidence and relationship are already in place.

Next, choose a loan officer (LO) who is a good match, both in culture and skill, for each branch. I can't stress strongly enough how important this is —I have seen mortgage affiliations fail time and again simply because the "match" wasn't right. Spend time on this; consider skills, ethics, personality, generational factor, and the ability to "get the job done"—get this right, or mortgage capture will never be what it could be.

Most companies form a limited liability company (LLC), which involves creating a third company that partners the real-estate company and the lender. This LLC has a separate identity from the two companies that formed it, but the establishing companies (the RE company and the lender) share all business that flows through the LLC.

The new mortgage company (LLC) will have access to your database, and this will allow the follow-up for refinancing and other services. Depending on the number of sales, the share of profit is generally 50/50. If you begin with a smaller number of buyer-controlled sales, you may start the venture with a 40/60 profit share, allowing for the increase to 50/50 when production increases. Put the designated increase in the agreement from the start. Create a non-compete agreement that prevents the lender from taking away your database if the LLC venture fails.

## Improving Capture Rate

At the onset, management is to meet with the LO (loan officer) in order to determine current relationships within the office.

Take an office roster and have the LO assign a 1, 2, or 3 designation to each agent.

**1** signifies that this agent sends the LO most of his or her deals (i.e., whenever possible).

**2** signifies that this agent has given "lip service" to the LO (i.e., asked for business cards, etc.), but as yet has not used the LO for a transaction.

**3** signifies that the agent and the LO have no relationship whatsoever. This may be an agent who has alliances in other place and sees no need to change them. Take heart! A lot of LO's, as well as their companies, will not survive the recession—therefore, opportunity may knock before too long, after all.

Make sure the LO understands that the intention of this list is not a punitive one; rather, it is a place to start within the office. Target agents (decide on a number) within the number 2 group and decide how you will "go after" them.

Review this 1-2-3 assessment on a quarterly basis and chart the progress.

I have listed the basic services that I believe all in-house lenders should provide. (*See In-House Mortgage Services Checklist.*) Beyond these "necessities," the LO could take agents out for lunch to ask for their business. However, *approach this carefully,* seeking to discover which lenders agents currently use and what is most important to them in an LO. Take notes.

## Broker Support Role

The managing broker can also support this effort by asking the agent to give the LO a try, and then report back to the broker on what kind of a job the LO did. Such a suggestion is most effectively handled during one-on-one coaching meeting with the agent. For instance, *"Susie, could I get you to give our LO a try? I'd really appreciate feedback from an agent of your caliber."* Then it's up to the LO to wow both the consumer and the agent in order to generate future business.

Introduce the in-house LO introduced to any new or experienced agent when that agent joins the company (i.e., during orientation). New agents, in particular, will appreciate having someone in-house who can explain the mortgage process.

Have the in-house LO do all office finance training—ideally, on a monthly basis. This training has proved invaluable during this period of increased foreclosures and short sales, as well as the changes in mortgage rules and regulations.

*[Form follows.]*

### IN-HOUSE MORTGAGE SERVICES CHECKLIST

*Communication is key. Make sure that you keep the agent informed.*

- LO introduction to new sales associates
- LO new-agent finance training classes (once a month)
- LO LS/BCS recognition/backup approval calls
- LO attendance/feedback at sales meetings
- LO weekend rate sheet (e-mail and hard copy)
- LO voice-mail broadcast: market "lock/float" updates
- LO attendance at office social functions
- LO creation of new-listing "Three Ways to Finance" flyer for brochure (as needed)
- LO creation OH "Three Ways to Finance" flyers (once a week)
- LO thank-you gifts (flower to agent after every closing)
- LO responsibility of "credit recovery program" (in order to put buyer on path to home ownership)
- LO meetings (with broker twice a month)
- LO reviews of agent roster -1-2-3 assessment -with broker once a quarter
- LO creation of interactive lender presence on company website
- LO creation of lender information for business cards (depending on office culture)
- LO customer-service follow-up (calling every consumer after closing)
- LO measurement of capture rate (as a percentage of BCS)

## LO Accountability

You should coach the LO twice a month (at the beginning and middle of every month). The purpose of this coaching is twofold: It allows you to receive the LO's feedback and also to monitor that he or she is offering services in a consistent manner—to both consumers and agents. I recommend that the LO complete a tracking form and  bring it to each meeting, so that the discussion of each coaching session focuses on the most-recent transactions.

Develop a system by which the LO receives all transaction/loan info ASAP from staff. LO's timely receipt of this info is necessary in order for LO to effectively make backup mortgage calls and complete the tracking form for each coaching meeting.

**Backup Mortgage Calls**

The LO makes these calls to any agent who has just listed or just sold a property—LO needs to make these calls ASAP after the JL-JS. (*This is, of course, assuming that agent used another LO. Backup mortgage calls are an offer of back-up service and congratulations on the transaction; it is fine for LO to leave a voice mail if necessary.*)

A good script for a backup mortgage call might be:

*"Hi, Susie, this is Jane (LO). Congratulations on your listing/sale on (address)! If I can be of help let me know; I'm happy to do a backup mortgage approval if you haven't gotten one already. Just let me know . . . and again, congrats!"*

Remember, this is an offer of both service and recognition—as well as a reminder for back up approval, which is necessary on most transactions today given the liquidity issues most face.

*[Form for LO coaching follows.]*

# LO COACHING MEETING

Evaluate participation in sales meetings. *LO should always provide information of interest at every sales meeting (weekly).*

Preparation of a listing flyer ("Three Ways to Finance") for each office listing. *Assess timeliness of listing flyer preparation. LO Must email the flyer to the agent no more than twenty-four hours after listing taken.*

Preparation of OH flyers. *Assess timeliness of OH flyer preparation. LO must give OH flyers to agent by Friday. LO can also "sit" OH and pre approve buyers. This offers "on-site lender" for the OH.*

Evaluate training classes. *Assess how many finance trainings LO held and attendance at each.*

Evaluate customer-service follow-up.

*Assess LO's consistency of backup/recognition calls for each BCS.*

What is your ratio—percentage of pre-approvals to loan applications to closed loans? What adjustments are you making to improve?

How many loans closed this month? How many of them closed on time?

What challenges are you experiencing?

## Settlement Services: Title/Escrow

These services vary by state. This business is earned by your affiliate based on the service and results they provide.

**"Legal Lunch"**—to increase settlement/escrow usage, hold this lunch once per month. An attorney would attend for an hour or two, and over lunch (attorney provides), would discuss current legal changes/issues/rulings and challenges. It's standing room only—agents love legal. It's a great way to build business for settlement/escrow and train your agents at the same time.

In states where attorneys are not the norm, escrow can still sponsor similar workshops, including foreclosures, short sales, etc.

You can also put together programs that promote **guarantees** when the consumer uses both mortgage and title. I like the idea of "guaranteed settlement costs and settlement dates"—such guarantees promote a standard of performance, with a financial penalty if not delivered. It's about time we put our money where our mouth is!

I can never say it enough: Nothing will substitute for doing the job well—and exceeding consumer and agent expectations.

Always, always stay up-to-date with RESPA changes! Given the mess we are in as of the time of this writing, regulations are going to tighten—"coloring within the lines" is something we all need to do.

# Epilogue

People often ask me which type of real-estate company model will emerge as the clear leader. Does one way of doing business have an advantage over another?

Full service, limited service, or online model—none of this is really the point. Consumers have diverse preferences—and they want **options.** *It is plausible that each of these models can survive, but only if each gives consumers what they are willing to pay for—and even then,* **only if each can still make a profit.**

As an industry, we have to look forward, rather than backward. We have to anticipate the consumer - figure out what they want, and then train like crazy in order to ensure consistent delivery. I have yet to discover a company that has created something new and original, *and* delivered it consistently. How many of us are waiting for the market to return to "normal"? The market we are in *is* normal, and it's our job. Shadow inventory promises to keep it challenging for another 4-5 years.

Opportunities abound. For company owners and management, it is a well-defined consumer-centric program, or system "map," which can guide an agent through this market; furthermore, it is highly skilled management that will implement it Monday through Friday. It's no longer about commission split; it's about the ability to earn a living—and companies must be able to show an agent exactly what they offer to ensure production, provided the agent follows the program. Without a program in place, no earthly reason exists for an agent to affiliate with a company.

It's about management and agents together understanding that true competitive advantage comes from getting measurable results for the consumer. It's about the numbers that measure results: Percentage of LS versus LT; DOM; percentage of actual sales price versus original list price; per-person production; number of days it takes a new agent to produce; lead-conversion rate; mortgage/settlement capture rate. If we want agents and consumers to listen to our counsel and advice, we need to use the numbers. The numbers measure, and so they back us up. To put it another way, these numbers verify our ability to "get the job done!"

Whatever the future holds, the well-trained and highly skilled companies that readily respond to the consumer— these are the companies with an assured future . . . no matter the market conditions.

# About the Author

Nancy Gardner has been a real estate professional since 1979. Nancy has been a national speaker, executive coach and trainer since 1997. She has successfully coached hundreds of real estate owners, general managers, and managers in the practical basics of running strong, competitive and profitable companies throughout the United States and Canada. Her clients range from single office companies to large multi branch operations. These companies include Independents, Franchised, Traditional and 100% models. Nancy works in all aspects of real estate brokerage operations: value based recruiting and retention; planning, coaching, training and implementation; ancillary services and mergers and acquisitions.

www.ngardnergroup.com